The Brain

by

Alexander Blade

The Brain
by Alexander Blade

Copyright © 2023

All Rights reserved.

No part of this publication may be reproduced, stored in a retrieval system, or transmitted in any form or by any means, electronic, mechanical, photocopying or Otherwise, without the written permission of the publisher.
The author/editor asserts the moral right to be identified as the author/editor of this work.

ISBN: 978-93-59326-83-2

Published by

DOUBLE 9 BOOKS

2/13-B, Ansari Road
Daryaganj, New Delhi – 110002
info@double9books.com
www.double9books.com
Tel. 011-40042856

This book is under public domain

ABOUT THE AUTHOR

Alexander Blade is a pseudonymous or lesser-known author who may have contributed to various genres or literary works. While not widely recognized in the literary world, authors like Alexander Blade often bring unique perspectives and creativity to their writing. They may specialize in niche genres, experimental styles, or emerging literary forms that have yet to gain mainstream attention. Authors who choose to use pseudonyms sometimes do so for privacy reasons or to explore different themes and styles outside their primary body of work. It's worth noting that the realm of literature is diverse and encompasses a wide range of voices, including those who may not have achieved widespread fame but nonetheless contribute to the rich tapestry of storytelling. Readers and literary enthusiasts often appreciate discovering hidden gems and emerging talents in the world of literature. Exploring the works of lesser-known authors like Alexander Blade can lead to exciting and unexpected literary experiences, showcasing the depth and diversity of the written word.

CONTENTS

CHAPTER I

Cautiously the young flight engineer stretched his cramped legs across some gadgets in his crowded little compartment. Leaning back in his swivel chair he folded a pair of freckled hands behind his neck and smiled at Lee.

America's greatest weapon, greater than the Atom Bomb, was its new, gigantic mechanical brain. It filled a whole mountain—and then it came to life...!

"This is it doctor; we're almost there."

The tall and lanky man at the frame of the door didn't seem to understand. Bending forward he peered through the little window near the engineer's desk, into the blue haze of the jets and down to the earth below, a vast bowl of desert land gleaming like silver in the glow of the sunrise.

"But this couldn't possibly be Washington," he finally said in a puzzled tone. "Why, we crossed the California coast only half an hour ago. Even at 1200 miles an hour we couldn't be almost there."

The engineer's smile broadened into a friendly grin: "No, we're not anywhere near Washington. But in a couple of minutes you'll see Cephalon and that's as far as we go. One professor and 15 tons of termites to be flown from Wallabawalla Mission station, Northern Territory, Australia, to Cephalon, Arizona, U.S.A., one way direct. Those are our instructions. Say, this is the queerest cargo I've ever flown, doctor, if you don't mind my saying so."

Lee blinked. Removing his glasses which were fairly thick, he wiped them carefully and put them on again as if to get a clearer picture of an unexpected situation. His long fingered hand went through his greying hair and then down the cheek which was sallow, stained with the atabrine from his latest malaria attack and badly in need of a shave. His mouth formed a big "O" of surprise as nervously he said:

"I don't get it. I don't understand this business at all. First the Department of Agriculture extends an urgent letter of invitation to a completely forgotten man out there in the Never-Never land. Then almost on the heels of the letter the government sends a plane. I would have been glad to mail to the Department samples of "Ant-termes Pacificus" sufficient for most scientific purposes if they needed them for experiments in termite control; that would have been the simple and the sensible thing to do. But no, they want everything I have; you fellows drop out of the sky with a sort of habeas corpus and a whole wrecking crew. You disturb the lives of my species, which took me ten years to breed; you pack up their mounds lock, stock and barrel. And then you drop me at some place I never even heard about—Cephalon. What is this Cephalon, anyway? If the place had any connotations to entomology, I would have known about it...."

The flight engineer glanced at the irritated scientist curiously and sympathetically: "If you don't know, I couldn't tell you what it's all about myself, I'm sure," he said slowly. "Cephalon—Cephalon is a place alright, but it doesn't show on the map. Sort of a Shangri-la, if you know what I mean."

This cryptic statement failed to have a calming effect on Lee. "Nonsense," he frowned. "If it is an inhabited place it must be on the map and if it isn't on the map the place doesn't exist."

"Look here," the flight engineer pointed through the window to the horizon ahead. "What do you think this is, doctor, a mirage?"

Lee stared at the apparition which swiftly materialized out of the ground haze at the plane's supersonic speed. "It *does* look like a mirage," he said judiciously. "Is that Cephalon?"

The engineer nodded. "Prettiest little town in the U. S. for my money. Ideal airport, too. Rather unusual though—I mean the architecture. Take a good look while we're circling around for the come-in signal."

Pretty and unusual were hardly the words for it, Lee thought, as he gazed in admiration. Below, Cephalon spread like a visionary's dream of a far-away future blended with a far-away past. Along wide, palm shaded avenues the flat-roofed terraced houses fanned out into the desert. Style elements of ancient Peru and Mexico were blended together with the latest advances of technology, such as the rectangular sheets of water which covered and cooled the roofs. The business center, dotted with helicopter landing fields on top of the pyramidal buildings, was reminiscent of the classic Babylon and Nineveh. At the center of the man-made oasis a huge fortress-like structure sprawled and towered like a seven-pointed star. Even so, for all its impressiveness of masonry, the lush green of its parks, the bursts of color from its hanging gardens, made Cephalon resemble one enormous flower bed.

Overawed and mystified the lone passenger from Down-Under took in the scene while the big plane circled with diminished speed. "It's beautiful," he murmered. "It's a dream." And louder then: "Pardon me if I find it hard to trust my senses. I've been away from home for more than ten years, to be sure. But then, even in the Australian bush I've received some periodicals and scientific journals from the U.S.A. Surely if a city like this has been built during my absence there should have been mention of the fact. And surely a city like this must show on some map. I don't understand. The longer I look the less I understand...."

The flight engineer shrugged. "It's a new city, maybe that's why it doesn't show."

Lee nodded. "In that case you must know the meaning of all this. Why did they build this city in the middle of the desert? What purpose does it serve? Why am I here? Why are we circling for so long? There don't seem to be any other planes up in the air."

"We cannot come in until our cargo has been examined and okayed," the engineer said.

Lee raised a pair of heavy and untidy brows: "Cargo examination? In mid-air and with nobody from the ground examining it?"

"That's it. It's being done by Radar, one of the new fangled kinds, you know." He grinned: "I hope, doctor, that your termite species is neither explosive nor fissionable in any way. Because in that case we could never make a landing in Cephalon."

"How utterly absurd," Lee said disgustedly. "Even a child would know better. There is no war going on—or is there? What makes them take such absurd precautions?"

The engineer narrowed his eyes. "You're an American, Dr. Lee, aren't you? Well, in any case, I can see no reason why I should be beating about the bush. After all, every foreign agent in this country must have learned by now about the existence of Cephalon. It's too big to be secret anyway. Besides, as you perceive, no attempt has been made to camouflage the place. Cephalon and the whole district takes up about a thousand square miles. It's a military preserve. Only you don't see any Brass. What they are doing, I wouldn't know, but I would rather try to rob all the gold from Fort Knox than get away with a single scrap of paper from that Braintrust Building in the center of the city over there. By the way, that skull shaped building right across the Plaza is the official hotel reserved for very important persons, such as you are listed."

A deep-throated buzz over the intercom interrupted him. "There, thank God, they finally made up their minds to let us in. One minute more and then a shower, a shave, bacon and eggs, and lots of Java!"

There were what appeared to Lee to be a multitude of people waiting as they landed. Eager and intelligent white faces all lifted up to him and pressed forward with bewildering offerings and requests. A Western Union messenger handed him a telegram in which one Dr. Howard K. Scriven proffered greetings, expressing a desire to interview him. Some cleancut youngster, obviously a scientific worker, assured Lee that he was fully familiar with the care and feeding of "Ant-termes-pacificus-Lee", that Lee need not concern himself about their welfare, that the mounds would be immediately transferred to Experimental Station 19 G. The "Flying Wing's" supercargo and two truck-drivers came forward with papers for Lee to sign, as the first of the heavy steelboxes which harbored the mounds were lowered into a van with the whine of an electric hoist. Meanwhile somebody who said he was an assistant manager of the Cranium hotel informed Lee that reservations had been made for him and that he had a car waiting to conduct Dr. Lee to his suite. It was all very mysterious, but efficient. Feeling more and more like some prize exhibit handled without a will of its own on a whirlwind tour, Lee allowed himself to be whisked from the airport to the hotel. With the din of the jets still in his ears, overpowered by impressions which crowded his senses from all sides, he listened politely to the hotel manager's explanations of the sights without understanding a word of them.

There were flowers in his suite, the carpets were deeper, the bathtub was bigger, the towels piled higher, the breakfast more abundantly rich than anything Lee could remember in the 38 years of his life. "So this is America in 1960," he thought. "It must have advanced by leaps and by bounds over these past ten years."

He felt embarrassed because he had almost forgotten the uses of all those comforts, and at the same time deeply moved over the way they embraced him, him, the lost son, the voluntary exile who once had turned his back on them in despair and disgust. But why was all this? He had done nothing to deserve this kind of hospitality. Entomologists as a rule were not transported by magic carpets into Arabian Nights for modest achievements such as the discovery of a new species. All the things which had happened within the last 24 hours were riddles wrapped up in enigmas. Fatigued as he was he couldn't lie down, he was desperately resolved to get at the bottom of this thing.

There came a buzz from the telephone. A soft and melodious contralto voice announced that its carrier was Dr. Howard K. Scriven's secretary and would Dr. Lee be good enough to come over to the Braintrust Building to meet Dr. Scriven at 9:30 A.M.? Lee said that he would.

The distance across the Plaza was short enough, but as Lee entered the hall of the huge concrete pyramid he was reminded of Washington's Pentagon in wartime, for his progress was halted right from the start and at more than one point. He had to line up at the receptionist's, he was being checked over the phone, a pass was handed to him, and somebody, obviously a plain-clothes man, took him to the express elevator which shot him up to the 40th floor.

There, another plain-clothes man conducted Lee through a long carpeted corridor and up one flight of stairs to a steel door which slid open automatically at their approach. Sunlight was flooding through its frame as Lee followed the guard and the door closed noiselessly behind them.

The man from Down-Under took a deep breath. He had not expected this for it was not a stepping in, but rather a stepping out from a vast tomb into the light of day. This was the top of a huge pyramid, and was in an entirely different kind of world.

The terrace was laid with flagstones and landscaped like a luxurious country club. In its middle there arose a penthouse, low and irregularly shaped like some organic outcropping of native rock. It could hardly be said that it had walls, overgrown as was the stone by creepers and built into the shape of massive pillars. The structure seemed a kind of Stonehenge improved upon by America's late great architect Frank Lloyd Wright. There were birch shade trees around the house, the leaves whispering in the breeze. From some crevice in the rock came the peaceful murmurings of a spring. A meandering little brook criss-crossed the gravel path under Lee's feet. From a stone table which might have belonged to some Pharaoh there came the only incongruous noise in this bucolic idyll; it was the nervous ticking of a typewriter, which stopped abruptly at Lee's approach, and the melodious contralto voice he had already heard over the phone greeted him. "Oh—it's Dr. Lee from Canberra University, isn't it? I'm so happy to meet you. Please, do sit down. How was your trip? I'm Oona Dahlborg, Dr. Scriven's secretary."

Lee blinked. Out of this world as was this Stone Age cabin in the sky, even more so was the girl. He had a vivid image of American girls as they had been when he had left the States way back in '49; in fact, he had an all too vivid memory of at least one of them. His memory had been refreshed within the last hour at the airport, at the hotel, at the receptionist's, and it had been confirmed: they still wore masks instead of their true faces, they still were overdressed, overloud, oversexed, overhung with trinkets and their voices still resounded shrilly from the roof of their mouths.

This girl Oona Dahlborg was different. He raked his brains to find some concept which would express how she was different. The word "organic" came to mind; yes, as one looked at her one sensed a unity of being, a creatural whole compared to which those other girls appeared as artificial composites.

She was tall for a girl, the pure Scandinavian type, and she looked like a young Viking with the golden helmet of her hair gleaming in the sun. She wore a tunic, short, sleeveless and of classic simplicity, the kind of dress which once Diana wore. It revealed the splendor of her slender figure and stressed the length of her full white limbs. On the black of the tunic an antique necklace of large amber beads formed the only ornament. The bow or the spear of the great huntress whom she resembled so much would have looked more natural in her hands than the typewriter; even so, her every move showed perfect coordination of body and mind, a large surplus of vital energy carefully controlled. Had she turned to some different career she might easily have developed into some great athlete or else a great singer. Her beautiful voice had that rare natural gift of using the whole thorax for a vessel of resonance instead of merely the mouth.

It was this voice which fascinated Lee more than the strangeness of the scene, more than her beauty, more even than the things she said. It was like remembering some haunting melody, it transported him into the forgotten land of his youth. It made him feel happy except that suddenly he felt painfully conscious of his ill fitting suit, the emaciation of his body, the atabrine stains on the skin of his face, the wildness and the grey of his hair.

With the shyness of a boy, he accepted first the firm pressure of her hand and then a seat which was another piece of ancient Egyptian furniture.

"Dr. Scriven will be with you in a few minutes," she said. "Unfortunately he is a little delayed by an official visitor from Washington. The unexpected always happens over here. Meanwhile...."

She suddenly interrupted herself. The searching look of her deep blue eyes startled Lee by its directness. There was in it a depth of understanding and of sympathy which penetrated to his heart. He felt as if she already knew about him and knew everything. It lasted only a few seconds before she continued, but in a different, a warmer voice:

"I think we can drop the usual conventions," she said. "We know you, Dr. Scriven and I. We know your work as published in the journal of entomology. It is the work of a man of genius. You are not the kind of man whom I must entertain with the usual small talk about the weather, how you have enjoyed your trip, or whether you feel very tired—as you probably do—and all the rest of it. That is routine with most of our visitors; it's quite a relief to feel that I can dispense with it for once."

Lee had blushed under this frankness of compliment as if a decoration had been pinned to his breast. "Thank you, Miss Dahlberg, you put me at my ease. I've been out in the wilderness for so long that I've lost the language of the social amenities. I really feel like another Rip van Winkle. All this," he made a sweeping gesture, "is tremendously new and surprising to me. There are so many burning questions to ask...."

The girl gave him a smile of sympathy. "Of course," she said, "and I can imagine some of them. To begin with, we owe you an explanation and an apology for having used the methods of deception in getting you here. As you probably know by now the work we're doing here is closely connected with the National defense. Whether we like it or not, military secrecy forces us to use roundabout ways in contacting scientists who happen to work in some context with our field, especially if they live in foreign lands. That's why in your case we have used the good offices of the Department of Agriculture in bringing you here. Dr. Scriven feels terrible about this. He feels that to be lifted out from one desert just to be dropped into the middle of another must be a fierce disappointment to you. For this and all the disturbance of your work—can you manage to forgive us Dr. Lee?"

The sincerity in these regrets was such that Lee hastened to reply: "You don't owe me any apology, Miss Dahlborg," he reassured her. "Naturally it is impossible for me to see any connection between my work with ants and termites and the problems of National Defense. But I am an American; I wouldn't doubt for a moment the legitimacy of your call." The girl nodded: "Besides you have fought for your country in the second world war," she added. "And also you are the son of General Jefferson Lee of the Marines. You understand of course that we had you investigated before calling you here; do you mind very much?"

Again Lee blushed; this time even deeper than before. He squirmed in his seat. "No, I guess not. I suppose it's necessary. Now that I'm going to meet Dr. Scriven, who is he? I probably ought to know—forgive my ignorance."

"You really don't know about him?" The girl sounded surprised. "He's a surgeon. He's considered the foremost living brain-specialist. Remember the Nuremberg trials of the Nazi war criminals? Dr. Scriven did the post-mortems on their brains. He wrote a book that made him famous."

"Of course," Lee slapped his forehead. "Yes, but of course, how could I forget."

"Yes," she answered, "He was made the head of the Braintrust over here."

"What is the Braintrust? What does it do? What am I supposed to do here?" Lee asked eagerly.

The girl's smile was mysterious: "I think Howard would like to explain all that to you in his own way."

"Howard". The word struck Lee like a vicious little snake. Was he a friend, or more than a friend to her? "This is terrible," he thought, "I've been away from normal life for overlong. Must be that I'm emotionally unbalanced. I haven't known her for five minutes. There is nothing between us. I've no earthly right to be jealous; it is absurd, it's mean."

He felt deeply ashamed. Yet as he looked at her he couldn't deny the truth before himself: that he *was* jealous, that he *had* fallen in love with a girl who looked like the goddess Diana with a golden helmet for hair.

There was a noise of footsteps on the gravel paths. A man with a portfolio under his arm walked briskly by the stonetable; despite his civilian clothes he had "Westpoint" written all over him. He disappeared through the steel door.

"That was General Vandergeest", Oona said. "Dr. Scriven will see you now; just walk in, Dr. Lee."

CHAPTER II

Inside, the cabin in the sky seemed to be built almost entirely around a huge primeval looking fireplace. Despite the fierceness of the Arizona sun there was a fire in it of long and bluish flames, one of those modern inventions which reverse the processes of nature. Like the gas refrigerators of an older period, this fire worked in combination with the airconditioning system to *cool* the house, lending to it in the midst of summer heat the same attractions which it had in winter.

In front of the fire and framed by its rather ghostly light, there stood a man with his head bowed down, pensively staring at the flames. As Lee's steps resounded from the ancient millstones which formed the floor, Dr. Scriven wheeled around; he approached the man from Down-Under with outstretched hands.

Rarely had Lee seen such a distinguished looking figure of a man. He looked more like a diplomat of the extinct old school than a scientist, with the immaculate expanse of his white tropical suit and the dignity of his leonine head. His width of shoulder and the smooth agility with which he moved gave the impression of great strength. Only his fingers were small, slender, almost like a woman's.

The reluctant softness of their pressure contrasted so much with his heartiness of manner that Lee felt repulsed by their touch until he remembered that a great surgeon lived and caused others to live by his sensitivity of hand.

"Dr. Lee, I'm happy, most happy, that you have been able to come." Scriven's voice was soft, but he spoke with an extraordinary precision of diction which had a quality almost of command. "Over there, please, by the fire...."

From the blue flames there came the freshness and the coolness of an ocean breeze; the rawhide chairs, built for barbaric chieftains as they seemed, proved to be most comfortable; the semidarkness, the roughness of the unhewn stone, gave a sense of the phantastical and the paradox. Lee sat and waited patiently for Scriven to explain.

"In case you're wondering a little about this setup," Scriven made a sweeping gesture around the room, "I've long since reached the conclusion that in these mad times a man needs above all some padded cell, some shell in which to retire and preserve his sanity. This is my padded cell, soundproof, lightproof, telephoneproof; a wholesome reminder of the basic, the primeval things. Simple, isn't it?"

Lee blinked at the extravagance of this statement. "Do you really call that simple?" he asked.

Scriven grinned: "You are right; it is of course a willed reversal from the complex, synthetic and perhaps a little perverse. But then, not everybody has the opportunity you had in living in the heart of nature. Frankly I envy you; your work reflects the depth of thinking which comes out of retirement from the world. That's why I called you here; that's why I am so sure you'll understand."

He paused. Lee thought that he saw what was perhaps a mannerism; the great surgeon didn't look at his visitor. With his head turned aside, staring into the flames, stroking his chin, speaking as if to himself, he reminded Lee of some medieval alchemist.

"It's a long story, Lee," Scriven continued. "It starts way back with a letter I wrote to the President of the United States. In this letter I pointed to the immense dangers which I anticipated in the event of an atom war; dangers to which the military appeared to be blind. I am referring to the inadequacy of the human brain and its susceptibility to mental and psychic shock. I explained how science and technology over the past few hundred years had developed by the *pooled* efforts of the *elite* in human brains, but that the individual brain, even if outstanding, was lagging farther and farther below the dizzy peak which science and technology in their totality had reached. I further explained, by the example of the Nazi and Jap States, how the collective brains of modern masses are reverting from and are hostile to a high level of civilization because it is beyond their mental reach. You know all this, of course, Lee. I made it clear that not even the collective brains of a general staff could be relied upon for normal functioning; that no matter how carefully protected physically, they remained exposed to psychic shock with its resultant errors of judgment. How much less then could production and transportation workers be expected to function effectively in the apocalyptic horrors they would have to face...."

Lee's eyes had narrowed in the concentration of listening; his head nodded approval. He wasn't conscious of it, but Scriven took note of it by a quick glance. His voice quickened:

"That was the first part of my letter, Lee. I then came out squarely with the project which has since become the work of my life. I told the President that under these circumstances the most needed thing for our country's national security would be the creation of a *mechanical* brain, some central ganglion bigger and better than its human counterpart, immune to shock of any kind. This ganglion to be established in the innermost fortress of America as an auxiliary augmenting and controlling the work of a general staff. I gave him a fairly detailed outline of just how the thing could be done. There was really nothing basically new involved. Personally I have held for a long time that Man never "invents", that in fact it is constitutionally impossible for him to do so. Being a part of nature Man merely *discovers* what nature has "invented" in some form of its own a long time ago. Mechanical brains. Lord, we have had them in their rudiments for the past hundred thousand years, at a minimum. The calendar is one; every printed book is one; the simplest of machines incorporates one. And ever since the first mechanical clock started its ticking we have developed them by leaps and bounds!"

"And did the President react positively to this project?" Lee asked.

Scriven shook his head. "He did not."

Then he paused. Little beads of perspiration had appeared on his forehead; he wiped them away with a handkerchief:

"That year, Lee," he began again, "when the decision was pending and I could do nothing but wait, knowing that there was no other defense against the Atom Bomb, knowing that our country's fate was at stake—it made me grey, it came pretty close to shattering my nerve.... But *then*...." His body tightened, the small fist pounded the rail of the chair: "*... But then We BUILT THE BRAIN.*"

He said it almost in a triumphant cry.

Mounting tension had Lee almost frozen to his seat. Now he stirred and leaned forward.

"It actually exists? I mean it works? It is not limited to the analysis of mathematical problems but capable of cerebrations after the manner of the human brain?"

Scriven, with a startling change, sounded dry, very factual in a tired way as he answered: "I appreciate your difficulty of realization, Dr. Lee. The whole idea is new to you and I have presented it in a rather abrupt and inadequate way. In time, and if we get together, as I hope we will, you shall get visual impressions which are better than words. For the moment, just to give you a general idea and to prove that this is not a small matter, let me give you a few facts: Our first monetary appropriation for The Brain, as an unspecified part of the military budget, of course, was for one billion dollars. We have since received two more appropriations of an equal size."

Lee's gasp made a sound like a low whistle. With a depreciating gesture Scriven waved it away.

"While these funds could only cover the first stages in the construction of The Brain," he calmly went on, "we have been able to build a mechanical cortex mantle composed of ninety billion electronic cells. Considering that the cortex mantle of the human brain contains over 9 billion cells, this doesn't sound like much. Our synthetic or mechanical cells are a little better than the organic, natural cells, but not very much. So alone and by themselves their number would indicate only a ten times superiority of The Brain over its human counterpart. If that were all the result of our labors, a brain of, let's say, twice genius capacity, we would be a miserable failure. But then we *have* achieved a very considerable improvement in the *utilization* of the The Brain's cortex capacity. In the first place we have full control over the intake of thought impulses; and more important, we use multiple wave lengths in feeding impulses to The Brain and throughout all the impulse-processings. Even the human brain has some capacity of simultaneous thought on different levels of consciousness, but its range in this respect is extremely limited. The Brain by way of contrast operates on two thousand different wave lengths, which means that The Brain can process at least 2000 problems at one time. Finally, the absence of fatigue in The Brain makes operations possible for 20 out of the 24 hours of the day—the rest of the time we need for servicing and overhauling."

With apparent effort Scriven turned his face away from the blue flames. His dark brown eyes probed into Lee's as he summed up:

"All together, Lee, The Brain has now reached the approximate capacity of 25,000 first class human brains. You as a man of vision will understand what that means...."

Lee had his face upturned. The tension of thought gave to his features something of the ecstatic or the somnambulist. Slowly he said:

"The equivalent of twenty-five-thousand human brains—there is no comparison other than a God's...."

Striven had jumped from his chair. He started pacing the flagstones in front of the fire, whirling his mighty frame around at every corner with a sort of wrath, as if about to meet some attack.

"Yes, you are right," he almost shouted, "we hold that power; that power almost of a God's. And how we are wasting it."

"What do you mean?" Lee's eye-brows shot up. "You would not waste those powers once you have them. You would turn them to the most constructive use—the advancement of science, of humanity!"

Scriven froze in his steps. A cruel smile parted his lips; there was a gnashing sound of big white teeth. He pointed a finger at his visitor.

"Idealist, eh? That's what I thought I was ten years ago. That's what I had in mind with The Brain right from the start. As it has turned out, however, the Army, Navy, Air Force, and half a dozen other government departments, besieged The Brain for the solution of their "problems", some of them as destructive as warfare, others as insipid as the trend of the popular vote in some provincial primaries. Sometimes Uncle Sam even farms out the services of the Brain to aid some friendly foreign government—without that government's knowledge as to where the solution is coming from. To cut a long story short: What these fellows utterly fail to understand is that The Brain is not a finite mechanism like any other, but a mechanism which unendingly evolves and becomes richer in its associations by the material which is being fed into its cells. In other words; the Brain *learns*; consequently it must be *taught*, it must be given the wherewithal for its own self-improvement...."

Scriven halted his impatient step by the other's chair. His nervous fingers tapped Lee's shoulder: "And that is where you come in."

"Me?" Lee asked, startled. "What you just told me, Dr. Scriven, it will take me weeks to comprehend. At the moment I am at a loss to see how my work could connect...."

The surgeon's sensitive hand patted Lee's shoulder as if it were the neck of a shy horse. "You *will* comprehend—in just another moment."

He pressed a button; in the entrance to the cabin in the sky the girl appeared, like an apparition. She approached, her hair a golden halo, her tunic transparent against the glare of the summer day. "Yes?"

"Oona, *please*"

She seemed familiar with the boss' code. With a smile on her lips she walked over to one of the pillars, opened a hidden recess and brought out the Scotch and syphon using an Egyptian clay tablet for a tray. With surgical exactitude Scriven poured out a good two fingers for his guest and an exceedingly small one for himself. "Stay with us for a moment, Oona, please," he said. "I didn't tell you the idea behind my calling Dr. Lee; you might be interested."

Wordlessly she slid into a seat, attentive and yet fading somehow into the background, as if trying to remain unnoticed. In that she did not succeed. Her beauty was such that its very presence changed the atmosphere; it put Lee under a strain to keep his eyes off her. As to Scriven, he seemed to address her almost as much as he did Lee.

"You have met Dr. Lee, haven't you, Oona; but do you know *whom* you have met? He probably wouldn't admit it; nevertheless Dr. Lee is the most successful peacemaker on earth, I think. He has just put an end to the oldest war in this world between the two most venerable civilizations in existence. That war between the states of the ants and the states of the termites has been waged with never abating fury for millions of years—until Dr. Lee came along with the perfect solution of the eternal dispute. All he did was to crossbreed the belligerents and now we have "united nations", *Ant-termes-pacificus-Lee* which lives up to the spirit of its name. Elementary, isn't it?"

"So elementary," the girl said with ironical sweetness, "that the so-called peacemakers of the international conferences must have considered it below their dignity to stoop to it. How exactly did you do it; I mean the crossbreeding?"

Lee felt his cheeks burn; it was extremely irritating that this should happen to him every time Oona Dahlborg spoke to him, especially when it was in praise.

"It wasn't too hard," he said depreciatingly. "The main difficulty lay not with the termite queen nor with the furtive little king of the ants themselves. Biggest trouble was in getting the potential lovers together against the bulldog determination of their palace guards. To use force was out of the question. So I had to trick the guards, smuggle in the male and keep him hidden under the royal abdomen of his spouse."

She smiled amused. "What a perfect classic; the story of Romeo and Juliet all over—and with you in the role of the nurse."

Lee blushed still deeper at that. "Yes", he admitted, "I was very much reminded of that story and my role in it. Only I had to avoid the tragic end."

"And how did you avoid the Shakespearean end?"

"In the best cloak and dagger manner, Miss Dahlborg. First I made the guards drunk; that's easy enough with termites. Then I broke into the chamber where they keep the queen immured. I killed her legitimate consort and substituted my own candidate after having anointed him with the genuine termite smell. Finally I re-immured the pair. There are only little holes in the walls through which the royal family is serviced, they are never really in touch with their guards. That's why it could work."

"And thus they lived happy forever afterwards," the girl concluded.

"I'm afraid not, Miss Dahlborg," he said, "there is no such thing as happiness in the eternal gloom of termite society. But even if not happy, the match I brought about was definitely blessed. In due course I became godfather to 30,000 baby ant-termes; I've about 15 million now in different hybrid strains. Now that I have an inkling of the grandiose work you are doing over here I am ashamed to mention mine; it's very small, very insignificant and I still don't see where it comes in."

The girl seemed to cross out those words with an energetic move of her head. "No," she said, "your work is not small nor is it insignificant; it is great and contains the most intriguing possibilities."

"Ah!" Scriven interrupted. "I have been waiting for this. I knew that Oona would hit upon those intriguing possibilities; her's is an unspoiled intelligence; it penetrates to the core of things. Dr. Lee, let me begin at the beginning so you will understand just where you and your work connect with The Brain. The society of the higher insect states like bees and ants and termites constitutes the oldest and the most stable civilizations in this world. Human society by way of contrast has created the youngest and the most unstable civilization amongst higher animals. Throughout history we find collapse after collapse of civilization. Quite possibly civilizations higher than ours may have existed in prehistoric times. Right?"

Lee nodded assent.

"Fine. From that it follows that Man has much to learn from the society of the higher insects. Their ingenious laws and methods, their "spirit of the hive," the incredible renouncement of individual existence and individual advantage, their undying devotion to the race.... We must study those if ever we want to reach anything like stability in *our* society. We ought to model our civilization after theirs, especially now that we have this new species "*Ant-termes-pacificus*" which has renounced war. There is something basically wrong with the type of civilizations which Man builds and which ceaselessly devour one another. No doubt you see the third World War approaching inexorably just as I do; civilization forging ahead, for what? For the big plunge into suicide. It's sickening to think of it. Do you feel I'm right?"

Unconscious of himself Lee had arisen and paced the room. With his lean long-legged figure bending slightly forward and wild-maned head bowed down in thought he resembled a big heron stalking the shallows for prey.

Fascinated, Oona's eyes followed the two contrasting men as their paths criss-crossed like guards before some palace gate. She alone had kept her seat. It was with greater assurance than before that Lee now spoke.

"I can see eye to eye with you, Scriven, as to the wrongs of man-made civilization and its probable course. But I do not think it desirable that we should model human society after the insect states. Ingenious as it is, their system is the most terrifying tyranny I could imagine. Just think of it: they literally work themselves to death. Workers who have outlived their usefulness are either killed off, or else they become the bloated, living containers for the tribe's staple food."

"You, yourself, can see the similar trend in Man, today. Our production of new thought is lagging; not starting from the roots, it becomes superficial, cut off from the roots. The results? The curse of the Babylonian confusion of the tongues under which we live. We are rapidly becoming thought-impotent. Cerebral fatigue, dissociation of its nerve paths, emotionalism which rejects logic as "too difficult", mass idiocy and relapse to barbarism.... It is by our brains, it is by this highest evolution of matter that we have built this civilization of ours; and now our own brainchild proceeds with might and with main to destroy the very organ of its creation. Is that not irony supreme?

"Now we have The Brain, this truly superlative tool of 20,000 times human capacity. All we have to do now is to submit the various societies which nature has built: insect states, other animal states, Man and his state to the analysis of The Brain. Have their good and their bad features tested and compared. Let The Brain synthesize all the beneficial components, let it shape the pattern of a new civilization more enduring and better adapted to the nature of Man. And then abide by the laws which The Brain lays down. I need your aid, Lee. You have already made one most valuable contribution to "peace on earth" with your "*Ant-termes-pacificus*". This is your big chance to continue the good work; be with us, be our man."

In silence both men stood close to each other, eyes searching. All Oona Dahlborg could hear was their heavy breathing. Instinctively she crossed her fingers; never before to her knowledge had Scriven opened his mind with such reckless abandon—and to a perfect stranger at that. Her respect for the strange, the birdlike man from Down-Under skyrocketed.

"He really must be a great man," she thought, and, "Howard and he will be either fast friends or very violent enemies."

At last Lee's voice came, husky and highpitched with emotion: "I cannot conceive of a man-made superhuman intelligence. Neither can I believe that mankind could or should be *forced* into its happiness by an intelligent machine. But that's besides the point ... the idea is grandiose. It has the sponsorship of the government. You say that The Brain needs me. That makes it a duty; so here I am."

He stretched out his hand and felt the cautiously eager grip of the surgeon's sensitive fingers. The great man beamed. "Good," he said, "I knew you would. Oona, like a good girl—the glasses, yours too. This really deserves a toast."

The girl stepped between the two men. Handing Lee his glass she said: "Today you may follow only the call of duty; tomorrow it will be the call of love. I've never met any man who has not fallen in love with his work for The Brain."

"I think you are quite right in that, Miss Dahlborg," he answered, wondering vaguely exactly what her words meant, wondering also just how much his decision was inspired by the wish to see more of her.

They drank their toast in silence. Scriven then turned to the girl:

"Apperception center 36," he said. "Yes, I think 36 will be the best. Get in touch with Operations, Oona. Tell them I want 36 cleared for the exclusive use of Dr. Lee. Call Experimental; I want the whole batch of "*Ant-termes-pacificus*" transferred to Apperception 36 by tomorrow morning. Then—no, today is too late and Dr. Lee is tired, he needs rest—but tomorrow at 8 A.M. I want a car for him to go over to The Brain. Would that suit you, Lee?"

"Fine; but why a car? It's only a few steps...." He stopped, confused by the hearty laughter in the wake of his words.

"It's quite a few steps, Dr. Lee." Oona said, "you would be *very* tired before you got there; chances are that your feet wouldn't carry you that far."

"But this is the Brain Trust Building," he stammered.

"It is," Scriven answered, "but it houses only part of the administration, not The Brain. You wouldn't expect us to place a thing of such vital strategic importance in a skyscraper on a wide open plain as a landmark for every enemy?"

"No, I guess not." Lee said. "But since I'm briefed to go there, where is it?"

"That," Scriven frowned, "is a very reasonable and a simple question. Unfortunately, *I do not know*."

Lee felt a wave of red anger; it rose into his cheeks because he saw the sparks of frank amusement dancing in Oona Dahlborg's eyes. He opened his mouth to some bitter remark about this hoax when Scriven put a restraining hand upon his arm.

"This is no joke, Lee. I have planned The Brain, have in part designed it, seen it under construction for the past ten years, managed its affairs—but I don't know where it is and that's a fact."

He led his speechless guest to a lookout on the west side of the room. Beyond the lush, green oasis of Cephalon the desert stretched unbroken till on the far horizon the mountains of the High Sierra rose in a blue haze of scorching sun. His hand moved sweepingly from north to south.

"Over there," he said, "somewhere inside those mountains; that's where it is. But its location? Your guess is as good as mine. Take your choice of any of the mountains, attach a name to it; I've done so myself. One of them must be "The Cranium", but the question remains: which? There are people who know, of course; military intelligence, the general staff; but that," he shrugged his shoulders, "... isn't my department."

CHAPTER III

The Brain Trust car which took Lee out of Cephalon was a normal-looking limousine, a rear-engined teardrop like all the "60" models, slotted for the insertion of wings which most of the garages now kept in stock and rented at a small charge for cross-country hops. The only non-standard feature seemed to be the polaroid glass windows which were provided all around and not only in front.

"That's a good idea," Lee said adjusting the nearest ones, "they ought to have that on every car, all-round protection to the eyes."

"Think so, sir? Must be the first time you're driving out there," the young chauffeur said.

The car left the outskirts and the desert started to fly by as the speedometer needle climbed above the 100 mark. Lee sank back into his seat; the desert had no novelty for him and since the chauffer appeared not inclined to small talk he abandoned himself to thought.

His visit to his father had not been much of a success....

Time magazine had carried an item in its personal column, briefly stating that General Jefferson E. Lee, "the Old Lion of Guadalcanal," had retired from the Marines to Phoenix, Ariz.... Phoenix, the hotel desk had informed him, was only some 300 miles away and there was hourly service by Greyhound helicopter-bus.

So he had taken the ride, a taxi had brought him to the small neat bungalow, and there he had seen his father for the first time in years. It had been very strange to see him aged, the nut brown face a little shrunk. He had anticipated that much. But somehow he had failed to imagine the most obvious change; to see his father in civvies and even less to see him trimming roses with a pair of garden shears. It looked such an incongruous picture for a "Marines' Marine."

As he had come up the little path his father had looked up.

"So it's you, Semper." Slowly he had peeled off the old parade kid gloves without a change in his face. "Nice to see you," he had said. "Didn't expect to before I start pushing up the daisies from below. Where's your butterfly net?"

No, in character his father hadn't changed a bit. He still was the old "blood and guts" to whom an entomologist was sort of a human grasshopper wielding a butterfly net, and a son indulging in such antics a bit of a freak, a reproach to his father, a failure of his life.

Even so, he had led the way into the house and things had been just as he remembered them: the old furniture, pictures crowding one another all over the walls, on the unused grand piano—Marines in Vera Cruz, Marines in China, Marines in Alaska, in the Marianas, in Japan, at the Panama canal; Marines, Marines, Marines, wherever one looked, in ghostly parade. No, nothing had changed. It had been mainly jealously which had caused him to rebel against becoming another Marine, the first wedge which had driven him and his father apart.

"What are you doing now, padre?" he had asked.

"You've seen it. Nothing. Just puttering around. They've made me commander of the National Guard over here," and with a contemptuous snort, "—a sinecure; might as well have given me a bunch of tin soldiers to play with. What brought you here?"

Glad to change the subject Lee had told about Australia, had mentioned The Brain and the possibility of joining it. His father had not been pleased.

"Heard of it," he had grumbled. "Shows how the country is going to the dogs. Now they need machines to do their thinking with. If their own brains were gas they couldn't back a car out of the garage. So you're mixed up with that outfit; well—how about a drink?"

"Rather," he had answered, feeling the need for washing down a bitterness; thinking, too, that it might break the ice between him and his father.

And then there was that painful moment when they had stood, glasses in hand and remembered....

The selfsame situation fifteen years ago as the Bomb fell upon Hiroshima. He had been on convalescence furlough. They had been alone when the news came and there had been a drink between them just as now. And after the announcer stopped he had cried out hysterically like a child in a nightmare.

"Those fools, that's the end of civilization, that's no longer war."

"Shut up," his father had shouted, "how dare you insult the Commander in Chief to my face. Get out of here and *stay* out."

A highball glass had crashed against the floor. And that had been the end. He hadn't returned after the war.

Yes, it was most unfortunate that now, after so many years, they should read that memory in their faces; that it was only the glasses and not the minds which clicked.

They had put them down awkwardly with frozen smiles on their lips and his father had said:

"Sorry. But an old dog won't learn new tricks. Guess it's too late in the day for me and you to get together, son."

"It's never too late, Dad," he had wanted to say, but the words died on his lips.

So it had been the failure of a mission; but then it closed an old and painful chapter with finality and he was free to open a new leaf.

Lee looked ahead again. The speedometer needle trembled around the 150 mark. The sun drenched sand shot by, Joshua trees gesticulating wildly in the tricky perspectives of the speed, out-crops of rocks getting bigger now and more numerous, the road ahead starting to coil into a maze of natural fortresses, giant pillars and bizarre pyramids looking like the works of a titan race from another planet shone in unearthly color schemes of black and purple and amber and green. With the winding of the road and the waftings of the heat it was hard to make out a course, but the Sierra Mountains now were towering almost up to the zenith; like a giant surf they seemed to race against the car.

"Mind if I close the windows, sir?"

The chauffeur's question was rhetoric; he had already pushed a button, the glass went up and within the next second the inside of the car turned completely dark.

"Man," Lee shouted, gripping the front seat, "are you crazy?"

There suddenly was light again, but it was only the electric light inside the car. The blackout of the world without remained complete, and the speedometer needle still edged over the 150 mark.

"Crazy? I hope not." The chauffeur said it coolly; leaning comfortably back he turned around for a better look at his fare.

With mounting horror Lee noticed that he even took his hands off the wheel. Nonchalantly he lit a cigarette while the unguided wheel milled crazily from side to side and the tires screeched through what seemed to be a sharp S-curve. Still with his back to the wheel and in between satisfying puffs of his smoke he continued:

"It's quite O.K. sir; it's only that we're on the guidebeam now. This here car doesn't need a driver no more; it's on the beam."

"What beam?" Lee relaxed a little; it was the unexpectedness which had bowled him over. "What beam? And why the blackout?"

"Just orders," the young man said. "The Brain's orders and it's the Brain's beam. Seems to be new to you, sir; to me it's like an old story; read about it when I was a kid: how they blindfolded people who entered a beleaguered fortress. "The Count of Monte Cristo," it was called; ever heard about it? Pretty soon now we'll be stopped for examination before we enter the secret passage underground. Romantic isn't it?"

"Very much so," Lee dryly remarked. He continued to watch the behavior of the car with some misgivings. The controls appeared to be functioning smoothly enough and after a minute or so the brake pedal came down all by itself. Lee, with a breath of relief, saw the speedometer recede to zero.

But the doors would not open from the inside and as he tried them he found that they were locked. "What's the idea," he asked, "I thought you said we would be examined at this spot?"

"Bet they're at it right now," the chauffeur grinned. "I wouldn't know how they do it, but they get us photographed inside and outside, what we have in our pockets, what we had for breakfast this morning and the very bones of our skeletons. I pass through here maybe half a dozen times a day, still they will do it every time: take my likeness. Makes me feel like I was some darned movie star."

To Lee it felt uncanny to sit trapped and blindfolded in this "Black Maria" of a car while unseen rays and cameras went over him. He could hear a faint noise of steps, and muffled voices.

"Who are they?" he asked.

"Oh, that's only some boys from Intelligence or whatnot; that's nothing, that isn't The Brain. It will be all over in a moment—see—there we go again. Now we're entering the Labyrinth."

"The Labyrinth?"

Reticent as he had been in the beginning, the chauffeur now seemed to like Lee; he was proud to explain. "Queer, isn't it? They've got the damnedest names for things down here. Take them from anatomy, I understand. The

Labyrinth is supposed to be inside the ear; it leads inside in a roundabout way; it's the same here, it's a tunnel—see—down we go."

The soft swoosh of the gas-turbine turned into a muffled roar. The car accelerated at a terrific rate and from the way it swayed and dived it was clear that the tunnel spiralled downwards in steep serpentines. Lee gripped the holding straps; his every nerve was on edge and those edges were sharpened by the ominous fact that all the instruments on the dashboard had stopped functioning so that he couldn't even read the speed.

As if to make things still worse, the chauffeur had abandoned his post altogether. Stretching his legs across the front seat he reclined as if enjoying his easy chair at home by the fire place.

"It beats a roller coaster, doesn't it?" the chauffeur said. "Got me scared the first few times before I found out it was safe. Nothing to worry about, never you fear."

With his stomach throttling his throat, Lee asked, "How deep are we going underground?"

"That we are not supposed to know; that's why all the instruments are cut off. The other day I had a passenger, one of those weathermen, a professor. He laughed when I told him I didn't know how deep it was. Got a little doodad out of his pocket; aneroid barometer, or something, he said it was. But he got a surprise; in the first place the thing didn't work, so he said the whole tunnel was probably pressurized. In the second place he never got where he wanted to go. They stopped the car at the next control and shot him right back whence he came."

"But why?"

The chauffeur looked mysterious. "Seems The Brain doesn't like people with doodads in their pockets even if they mean no harm. The Brain is most particular about such things; maybe somehow it peers into this car this moment, maybe it records every word we say. How do we know?" He shrugged his shoulders. "Not that I give a damn. I've got nothing to conceal. The hours are right and the pay's right; that's good enough for me."

Lee experienced an old, familiar sensation: that creepy feeling one got on jungle patrol, knowing that there were Jap snipers up in the trees, invisible with the devilish green on their faces and uniforms.

"Strange," he thought, "that in the very center of civilization one should feel as haunted as in the jungle hell."

Then, just as he began to wonder whether the dizzy spiralling plunge as if in the belly of a shark would ever end, the tunnel levelled. Now the car shot straight as a bullet and just as fast it seemed.

As his stomach returned to something like normal position, the feeling of oppression changed into one of flying through space, of being dynamically at rest. Again just as the duration of this dynamic flight evoked the feel of infinity, the motion changed. So fast did it recede that the momentum of his body almost hurled Lee from the back seat into the front.

Doors snapped open and as Lee staggered out somewhat benumbed in limb and head, his eyes grew big as they met the most unexpected sight. The car rested on the concrete apron of what appeared to be a super-duper bus terminal plus service station and streamlined restaurant. Beyond this elevated terrace yawned a vaulted dome, excavated from the solid rock and at least twice the size of St. Peter's giant cupola. Its walls were covered with murals. Both huge and beautiful they depicted the history of the human race, Man's evolution. From where he stood they started out with scenes of primeval huntings of the mammoth, went on to fire making, fire adoration, then to the primitive crafts and from there through the stages of science evolution and technology until they ended on Lee's right hand side with an awesome scene from the Bikini test. The gorgeous mushroom cloud of the atomic explosion looked alive and threatening like those Djinni once banned by Solomon.

But then, all these murals looked more alive than any work of art Lee had ever seen and he discovered that this was due to a new technique which had been added and commingled with one of the oldest.

The pictures were built up from myriad layers of Painted Desert sands and these were made translucent or illuminated by what Lee thought must be phosphoric salts turned radiant under the stimulants of hidden lights. Whatever it was, the esoteric beauty of this jewel-like luminosity surpassed even that of the stained glass windows in the great cathedrals of France.

"Pretty isn't it? The chauffeur's words came as an anticlimax to what Lee felt. "That fellow over there in the middle; he's supposed to have it all thought out." He pointed to a collossal bronze statue which towered in the center of the cupola to a height of better than a hundred feet.

Raising his eyes to the head of this giant, Lee discovered that the figure was that of "The Thinker" by Rodin though it was cast in proportion its creator would not have deemed possible.

Completely overwhelmed and overawed by the grandeur of it all, Lee barely managed to stammer, "What—what is this place; what is it called?"

"It's kind of an assembly hall; the staff of The Brain have meetings over here at times. Besides it's sort of a Grand Central; transportation starts here at times throughout the Brain. But listen, they are already paging you."

Out of nowhere as it seemed there came a brisk, pleasant female voice.

"Dr. Lee, calling Dr. Semper F. Lee from Canberra University, please answer Dr. Lee."

The chauffeur nudged Lee in the ribs.

"Say something, she hears you all right."

"Yes, this is Lee speaking," he said in a startled voice.

The voice appeared delighted.

"Good morning, Dr. Lee: I'm Vivian Leahy of Apperception Center 27; I'm to be your guide on the way up. Now, Dr. Lee, will you please step over to the glideways. They're to your right. Take glideway T, do just as you would in a department store—" she giggled, "—stand on it and it will get you right to the occipital cortex area. I'll be waiting for you over there. I would have loved to come down and conduct you personally, but it's against regulations; I'll explain to you the reasons why in a little while. And if you have any questions while en route, just call out. So long, Dr. Lee; I'll be seeing you...."

Greatly bewildered by this gushing reception Lee found it hard to follow instructions, simple as they were. The array of escalators which he found in a side wing was a formidable one and confusing with movements in all directions, crisscrossing and overlapping one another. Despite the very clear illuminated signs Lee almost stepped upon glideway "P" when "the voice" warned him:

"Oh no, Dr. Lee; just a little to your left—that's fine, that's the one— there."

Obviously his loquacious guardian angel could not only hear him but watch his steps as well. Apart from being uncanny, this was embarrassing; feeling reduced to the mental age of the nursery, he gripped the rails of "T" which went with him into a smooth and noiseless upward slide. The shaft was narrow, there was little light at the start and it grew dimmer as he went. After a minute or so the darkness had turned almost complete and became oppressive. Simultaneously there was a disquieting change from the accepted normal manner in which escalators are supposed to move. Its rise gradually turned perpendicular and in doing so the steps drew apart. Before long Lee felt squeezed into some interminable cylinder, standing on top of a piston as it were, a piston which moved with fair rapidity along transparent walls. That these walls were either glass or transparent plastics he could perceive from objects which came streaking by with faint luminosity. They looked like columns of amber colored liquids in which were suspended what looked like giant snakes, indistinct shapes, but radiant in the mysterious manner of deep sea fishes. They almost encircled the transparent cylinder shaft in which Lee moved; there were many of them; how many Lee couldn't even attempt to guess. The swiftness of his ascent through these floating, waving radiances for which he had no name was nightmarish, like falling into some bottomless well. With great relief he heard the voice of his guide breaking the spell.

"I'm terribly sorry, Dr. Lee, I shouldn't have deserted you, there was some little interruption—" palpably the voice was tickled to death "—my boy friend called from another department and so ... you know how it is. Let's see, where are you? Good lord, already near the end of the Medulla Oblongata with the Cerebellum coming and I haven't told you a *thing*. Goody, where should I begin; I'm all in a dither: Well, Dr. Lee; most people seem to expect The Brain to be like a great big telephone exchange, but it really isn't that kind of a mechanism *at all*. We have found—" she sounded important as if it were her very own discovery "—that the best pattern for The Brain would actually be the human brain. So The Brain is organized in nearly identical manner, likewise our whole terminology is taken from anatomy rather than from technology. The glideways for instance, travel along the natural fissures between the convolutions of the various lobes; that's why they are so very winding as you will see as you enter The Brain proper. Those columns you see are filled with liquid insulators for the nerve cables to vibrate in; for they *do* vibrate, Dr. Lee, as they transmit their messages.

"You have noticed the narrowness of the glideways, the terrible confinement of space. I know it's horrible—many of our visitors suffer claustrophobia, but they just must be built that way. You see even fractions of a millionth of one second count in the coordination of the association bundles and nerve circuits, that's why everything is built as compact as possible, worse than in a submarine.

"Then, too, you must have wondered why everything is so dark inside. That's another thing wherein The Brain is like the human brain; its nerve cells are so extremely sensitive that they are distributed by light. We use black light almost exclusively or activated phosphorous such as on the sheaths of the nerve cables. For the same reason we of the personnel are normally not permitted to pass through the interior of The Brain during operations-time. Exceptions are only made in the case of very important persons such as you are. Normally one travels to one's stations through the ducts elevator shafts in the bone matter or rather the rock outside. Those are *so* much faster and more comfortable Dr. Lee; oh I feel *so* bad about you, poor man, traveling all alone through this *horrible* maze without a human soul in sight."

Lee grinned. He wouldn't have liked to be married to this chatterbox no matter how beautiful she might turn out to be; but at the moment her exceeding femininity was most comforting in the weirdness which surrounded him.

The little platform under his feet started acting up again in the queerest manner. It pushed him forward and the wall at the rear kicked him in the back; his nose flattened against the sliding cylinder in front as the contraption reverted from the perpendicular course to something like the undulations of a traveling wave. Lee darkly perceived group after group of luminous cables coiling away into cavernous pits filled with what looked like eyes of cats, faintly aglow and twinkling at him from the dark. They reminded him of the fireflies of the green hells he had been in during the war.

"You are now skirting the convolutions of the cerebellum," his guardian angel told him. "They are electronic tubes which receive sensory impressions and translate them into impulses for cerebration. Here in the cerebellum the bulk of the associations is being evoked; these are then distributed throughout the hemispheres of the cortex or higher brain. Oh I *do* wish you wouldn't get seasick, Dr. Lee; *some* of our visitors do, you know; it's those wavy, wavy movements."

The sympathetic Vivian came much too close to the truth for Lee to think her funny. With a sense of approaching disaster he stared at the sliding cylinder walls; from time to time the passing lights reflected his face, distorted and decidedly greenish in tint. Trouble was that seemingly nowhere there was any fixed point on which to stabilize the eye. He seemed to be carried on the back of a galloping boa constrictor with a couple of others streaking away under his armpits.

Some of the caves which he had skirted were alive with ruby electronic eyes and some were green and again there were others in which all the colors of the rainbow mixed. There was no end to them, nor could he gauge their depths. After an interminable time of this the glideway went into a flying upward leap. Again the perspective changed completely; now the thing seemed to be suspended from the ceiling with slanting views opening toward the scene below through its transparent sides.

"You are now passing across the commissures into the cerebrum," came Vivian's voice just as Lee thought that nausea was getting the better of him. "You'll now ascend along one of the main gyri through the mid-brain between the hemispheres. Those masses of ganglions below and coming from all sides as they go over the pass of the ridge are association bundles.

Beyond they disperse again over the cortex mantle to all the centers of coordination, higher cerebration and higher psychic activities. Things will be a little easier now for you, Dr. Lee; physically I mean. There *will* be some gyrations but not quite so *violent*. Oh you're holding out fine, like a real *He-man*, you're looking *swell* in my television screen."

Certain as he was that he looked rather like a scarecrow in a snowstorm Lee felt grateful for the praise. Besides she was right; the boa constrictor which he rode calmed down a little, marching with a dignity more in accordance with its size. Momentarily the luminous nerve cables, flying as they did toward him, threatened sudden death, however, they merely brushed the transparent cylinder, wrapping it up in a rainbow and then winged away again. Below acres of space streamed by, seed beds one could imagine to be young typewriters, millions of them, all ticking away with dainty precision, sparkling with myriads of tiny lights as they did.

Then there came more acres teeming with fractional horsepower motors; he could hear their beehive hummings even through the plexiglass. The things they drove Lee couldn't make out because the adjoining acres of this underground hothouse for mushrooming machines were again shrouded in darkness except for sparks which crossed the unfathomable expanse like tracer bullets. Struck with a sort of word blindness caused by the sensory impressions barrage, Lee could no longer grasp the meaning of Vivian's voice as it went on and on explaining things like "crystal cells," "selenoid cells," "grey matter pyramidal cells," powered somehow by atomic fission, "nerve loops" and "synthesis gates" which were not to be confused with "analysis gates" while they looked exactly the same....

Apart from this at least one half of his mental and physical energy had to be expanded in suppressing nausea and bracing himself against the gyrations which still jerked his feet from under him and made friction disks of his shoulders as his body swayed from side to side. All of a sudden he felt that he was being derailed. There was an opening in the plastics wall of the cylinder; a curved metal shield like the blade of a bulldozer jumped into his path, caught him, slowed down his momentum and delivered him safely at a door marked "Apperception-Center 24." It opened and within its frame there stood an angel neatly dressed in the uniform of a registered nurse.

"*There*," said the angel, "at *last*. How did you like your little Odyssey through The Brain, Dr. Lee?"

Lee pushed a hand through the mane of his hair; it felt moist and much tangled up.

"Thanks," he said. "It was quite an experience. I enjoyed it; Ulysses, too, probably enjoyed his trip between Scylla and Charybdis—after it was over! It's Miss Leahy, I presume."

The reception room where he had landed, the long white corridor, the instruments gleaming in built-in recesses behind crystal glass, the nurse's uniform; all spelled clinic, a private one rather for the well-to-do. Since the procedure was routine he might as well submit to it, Lee thought. He felt the familiar taste of disinfectant as a thermometer was stuck into his mouth and then the rubber tube around his arm throbbing with the vigorous pumpings of the efficient Vivian.

"L. F. Mellish, M.D.—I. C. Bondy, M.D." was painted on the frosted glass door where she led him afterward. The two medics received Lee with a show of respect mixed with professional cordiality. Both Bondy, the dark and oriental looking chap, and Mellish, blond and florid, were in their middle twenties and both wore tweeds which depressed Lee with the perfection of their cut. Seeing the professional table at the center of the office, Lee frowned but started to undress; he wanted this thing done and over with as soon as possible.

"No, no—that won't be necessary, Dr. Lee," they stopped him laughingly, "We have already a complete medical report on you. Came in this morning from the Queen Elizabeth Hospital in Canberra on our request. You're an old malaria man, Dr. Lee; your first attack occured in '42 during the Pacific campaign. Pity you refused to return to the States for a complete cure right then. As it is it's turned recurrent; left you a bit anemic, liver's slightly affected. But in all other respects you're sound of limb and wind; we've gone over the report pretty carefully."

"Then why bother with me at all?" Lee said irritably. He had been in doctors' hands too often and had become a little impatient of them.

The freckled hand of Mellish patted his arm. "We do things different over here," he said and Bondy chimed in. "Or rather The Brain does. Just lie down on that table, Dr. Lee, and relax. We're going to enjoy a little movie together, that's all."

Lee did as he was bidden, but hesitant and suspiciously. He hated medical exams, especially those where parts of one's body were hooked up to a lot of impressive machinery. Of this there obviously was a good deal. The two medics seemed determined literally to wall him in with gadgetry. From the ceiling they lowered a huge, heavy-looking disk; not lights, but more like an electro-magnet beset with protruding needles. Lee couldn't see the cables but hoped they were strong, for the thing weighed at least a ton and, overhanging him, looked much more ominous than the sword of

Damocles. They wheeled a silver screen to the foot of the table and batteries of what appeared to be thermo-therapeutic equipment to both sides. He wasn't being hooked up to anything, but there was much activity with testing of circuits, button-pushings and shiftings of relay-levers. And then all of a sudden lights went out in the room.

"Say, what is the meaning of all this?" Lee raised his head uneasily from the hard cushion. All he could see now were arrays of luminous dials and the faint radiations from electronic tubes filtering through metal screens inside the apparatus which fenced him in. From behind his head a suave voice—was it Bondy's or Mellish's answered out of the dark.

"This is a subconscious analysis and mental reactions test, Dr. Lee. It's an entirely new method made possible only by The Brain. It has tremendous possibilities; they might include your own work as well."

"Oh Lord," Lee moaned. "Something like psychoanalysis? Have you got it mechanized by now? How terrible."

There was a low chuckle from the other side of his head; they both appeared to have drawn up chairs beyond his field of vision. Lee didn't like it; he liked none of it, in fact. He felt trapped.

"No, Dr. Lee," said the chuckling voice. "This isn't psychoanalysis in the old sense at all. You are not exposed to any fanciful human interpretation, and it isn't wholly mechanical either as you seem to think. The Brain is going to show you certain images and by way of spontaneous psychosomatic reaction you are going to produce certain images in response. Results are visual, immediate and as convincing as a reflection in a mirror; that's the new beauty of it. And now, concentrate your mind upon your body. Do you feel anything touching you?"

"Y-e-s," Lee said, "I think I do—it's—it's uncanny: it's like spiders' feet—millions of them. It's running all over my skin. What is it?"

"I think he's warming up," whispered the second voice; then came the first again.

"It's feeler rays, Dr. Lee; the first wave, low penetration surface rays."

"Where do they come from?"

"From overhead; that is, from the teletactile centers of The Brain."

"What do they do to me?"

There was the low chuckle again. "They excite the surface nerves of your body, open up the path for the deep-penetration rays; they proceed from the lower organs to the higher ones; in the end they reach the conscious levels of your brain. It's the tune-in as we call it, Dr. Lee."

A small movie projector began to purr; a bright rectangle was thrown upon the silver screen and then, Lee stirred. Hands, soothing but firm held him down. "Where did you get *those*." he exclaimed.

"From many sources," a calm answer came, "The papers, the newsreels, the War-Department, old friends of yours...."

What was unrolled on the silver screen were chapters from Lee's own life. They were incomplete, they were hastily thrown together, they were like leaves which a child tears from its picturebook. But knowing the book of his life, every picture acted as a key unlocking the treasures and the horrors amassed in the vaults of memory. It began with the old homestead in Virginia. Mother had taken that reel of the new mechanical cotton picker at work. There it was, a great big thing with the darkies standing around scratching their heads. There he was himself, aged twelve, with his .22 cal. rifle in hand and Musha, the coon dog, by his side; Musha, how he had loved that dog—and how he had cried when it got killed.

Pictures of the Alexander Hamilton Military Academy. Some of the worst years of his life he had spent behind the walls of that imitation castle.

The bombs upon Pearl Harbor.... He had enlisted the following day. On his return from the induction center mother had said.... Her figure, her movements, her voice loomed enormous in his memory.... But now the pictures of the Pacific War flicked across the screen.... They were picked from campaigns in which he, Lee had participated. They were also picked from documentaries which the government had never dared to let the public see ... close-ups of a torpedoed troop carrier, capsizing, coming down upon the struggling survivors in the shark-infested sea. It had been his own ship, the *Monticello*, but he had never known that an automatic camera had operated in the nose of the plane which had circled the scene....

Port Darwin—Guadacanal—Iwo Jima: close-ups of flame throwing tanks advancing up a ridge. He had commanded one of them.... Antlike human figures of fleeing Japs and the flames leaping at them.... So vivid was the memory that the smell returned to his nostrils, the sickening stench of burning human flesh. It tortured him. His voice was husky with revulsion as he said:

"What's the good of all this; take it away."

"Oh, no," one of the medics answered. "We couldn't think of that. We've got to see this to the end. What are your physical sensations now, Dr. Lee?"

"It's fingers now—soft fingers. They are tapping me from all sides like—like a vibration massage. It's strange though—they're tapping from the inside—little pneumatic hammers at a furious pace. They seem to work upon my diaphragm for a drum. But it doesn't pain."

"Good, very good; that was a fine description, Lee. That burning city was Manilla wasn't it, when MacArthur returned? You were in that second Philippine campaign too weren't you, Lee? That was when you won the Congressional Medal of Honor."

Yes, it was Manila all right, and there was Mindanao where the Japs had put up that suicide defence of the caves.

Lee's battalion had been in the attack; steeply uphill with no cover, it had been murder.... And seeing his best men mowed down, he had turned berserk. He had used a bulldozer for a battering ram, had driven it single handed directly into the fire-spitting mouth of the objective, raising its blade like a battle-axe. An avalanche of rocks and dirt had come down from the top of the cave under the artillery barrage and he had rammed the stuff down into the throat of the fiery dragon, again and again. He never rightly knew he did it. It had all ended in a blackout from loss of blood. It had been in a hospital that they pinned that medal on him which he felt was undeserved....

Now the reel showed him what at the time he hadn't seen; the end of the battle for the Philippines: Pulverised volcanic rock seen from the air, battle planes swooping down upon little fumaroles, the ventilator shafts of caves defeated but still unsurrendered. Big, plump canisters plummeted from the bellies of the planes. And then the jellied gasoline ignited, turning those thousands of lives trapped in the deep into one vast funeral pyre.... For over fifteen years he had tried to forget, to bury the war, to keep it jailed up in the dungeon of the subconscious. Now those accursed medics had unleashed the monster of war and as it stared at him from the screen it had that blood-freezing, that hypnotic effect which the Greeks once ascribed to the monstrous Gorgon.

Mellish's voice—or was it Bondy's?—seemed to come through a fog and over a vast distance as it asked: "What seems to be the matter, Lee? You're sweating, your body shakes; what do you feel?"

"It's those rays," he tried to defend himself. "It's the vibrations—the fingers. They are gripping the heart; it's like the whole body was turned into a heart. It's like another life invading mine—it's ghostly. Stop it, for heaven's sake."

"Not yet, Lee, not yet. Everything's under control, you're reacting beautifully; you're really feeling fine, Lee, just fine."

"If only I could get at his throat," Lee thought. "I would squeeze the oil of that voice and never be sorry I did." He tried to stir and found that it couldn't be done; every muscle seemed tied in a cataleptic state. Then he heard the other medic speak.

"You were shown this little movie Lee in order to stimulate your mind into the production of a movie of its own. You have responded, you have answered the call. While you saw the first, the sensory tactile rays working in five layers of penetration have recorded and have carried your every reaction to The Brain. The Brain, in a very real sense has read your mind and it has retranslated these readings into visual images. We are now going to watch the shapes of your own thoughts. Here we go...."

The projector which had stopped for a minute began to purr again. As the first thought-image jumped upon the screen there was a low moan of amazement mixed with acute pain. It escaped Lee's mouth, uncontrollably as the abyss of the subconscious opened and he saw:

A monstrous animal shaped like an octopus crawling across a cotton field. Nearer and nearer it crept, enormous, threatening; and suddenly there was a sharp excited bark and a spotted coon dog raced across the field toward the monster. He heard the voice of a small boy whimpering: "Musha, oh Musha, don't, *please* don't." But the dog wouldn't hear and the monster flashed an enormous evil eye, just once and then it gripped the dog with its tentacle arms tearing its body apart, chewing it up between horrible sabre teeth.... As through an ether mask he heard the two medics say: "That must have been a considerable shock to him," and "With a sensitive nature like that, and at that sensitive age, such an impression becomes permanent."

The Alexander Hamilton Military Academy appeared, not real, yet more than real. It was a narrow court yard surrounded by huge walls slanting toward the inside; it was huge and forbidding, fortress-towers standing guard, it was enormous gates forever barred, it was the figure of a huge Marine pacing fiercely back and forth in front of those gates, the same ghostly Marine watching all gates so that nobody could escape....

"That's probably his father," the voices whispered behind his ears. "Yes; the archetype. He'll bring up the Mother, too, I'll bet...."

As in those paintings of the primitives where kings and queens are very tall and common folks are very small, Lee saw her now: Mother. That had been just after induction when he had brought her what he thought was joyous news. Her face filled the whole screen. It looked as if composed from jagged ectoplasms, quite transparent except for the eyes. Deep and burning with pain they were, boring into his own. And there was smoke coming out of her mouth and it formed words: "But, Semper, you are still a child. One mustn't use children for this sort of thing; one mustn't." Every letter of these smoke-written words seemed to be flying toward him on wings....

"Terrific," the voices murmured at Lee's back. "Remember the case history? She died of cancer six months after he went overseas." "Yes, I remember; he's never seen her again. He's probably built up a strong complex out of that one, too."

On the screen now danced images almost totally abstracted from the realities of the filmed documentaries from the war.

They were whirling columns of smoke; they were like the vast, dark interior of a huge thunderhead cloud through which a glider soars, illuminated only by the flashes of lightning as for split seconds they revealed a fraction of some horrible reality: A burning ocean with screaming human faces bobbing in the flames. The whirling tracks of a tank going across some writhing human body and leaving it flat in its tracks, sprawling like an empty coat dyed red. And then the swirling, howling darkness closing in again....

"Interesting eh?" A voice broke through his cataleptic trance and the other answered: "Beautiful; almost a classical case. Great plasticity of imagination." "Yes; that's exactly what sets me wondering; the fellow should have cracked up by all the rules of the game." "How do we know that he hasn't? Maybe he was psycho and they didn't notice; they had some godawful asses for psychiatrists in war medicine. It's quite a possibility; well, his image production is ebbing now; I don't expect anything new of significance, what do you think?" "Now; we've got what we wanted anyway. Let's take him out of it; but go easy on the rheostats."

The projector stopped. The masterful, the ghostly fingers which had been playing on the keyboard of his mind very slowly receded from a furious fortissimo to a pianissimo. At first only the flutterings of the diaphragm eased, then the violent palpitations of a foreign pulse slipped off the heart; the liberated lungs expanded; tremors were running through the body as through the ice of a frozen river at spring; and then at last the mind escaped from its captivity.

Gradually as in a cinema after the show the lights reappeared. Blinking, Lee stared at the man who stood over him taking his pulse; it was Bondy. Mellish stood at the foot of the table with his back to Lee; he seemed to watch some apparatus which made noises like a teletype machine. Swinging his legs off the table Lee said:

"I'm okay; you needn't hold my hand."

But then he noticed that he wasn't. His head spun, his whole body was wet with perspiration, he felt very weak and limp. He swayed and buried his face in his hands trying to gain his balance, trying to shake off the trance. "Excuse me," he said. "I'm a bit dizzy."

As he opened his eyes again the two medics were standing right in front of him and smiling down on him with their bland, professional smiles. Lee felt the upsurge of intense dislike. He had seen those smiles before, often—too often: they seemed to be standard equipment with the medical profession whenever a fellow was about to be dispatched to the "table", or worse, to the psychopathic ward. Instinct told him that there was something in the air and also that his best bet would be a brave show of normalcy:

"This test, these new methods of psychoanalysis, they are extremely interesting," he said with an effort.

"Thank you, Dr. Lee," it was Mellish who spoke. "We knew you would find the experience worthwhile even if we put you under a considerable strain. A complete analysis in those olden days of Dr. Freud took three years; now thanks to The Brain we get approximately the same results within as many hours; that's some progress, isn't it?"

"Enormous," Lee said dryly while his eyes wandered over to Bondy; he knew the pattern, it would be Bondy's turn now to have a shot at him. There it came; and how he loathed the false heartiness of that voice.

"Dr. Lee, I'm afraid we have a bit of bad news for you—your test—the results have been negative. You have failed."

"Failed?" For a fraction of a second Lee's heart stopped beating. "In what sense? And what does that mean?"

Now it was Mellish's turn. "Dr. Lee, there must be frankness amongst colleagues and as a fellow scientist you'll understand. In the first place the decision isn't ours; we merely conduct the test on behalf of The Brain. The Brain, as you know, is the most highly developed machine in all the world. Its functions, its whole existence depend entirely upon the human skills and the human loyalties amongst its staff. A three-billion-dollar investment, plus the vital role of The Brain in our national defence, justify the extreme precautions which we are forced to take for its protection."

"What exactly are you driving at?"

"Please don't take it as an insult," now it was Bondy again. "There's nothing personal in this. It's merely that your emotional-reaction chart definitely shows a certain antagonism which from childhood-experience and war-experience you have built up against technology. It's nothing but a potential; it is confined to your subconscious. But even a potential danger of subconscious revolt is more than The Brain can risk amongst its associates. We fully appreciate the wish of our Dr. Scriven to enlist your very valuable aid, but...."

"I see" Lee interrupted, "but you would feel safer if I were to return to Australia by the next plane."

His head bent under the blow. A short 24 hours ago The Brain had been a nebulous, almost a non-existent thing. Since then a whole new world had been opened to him in revelations blinding and magnetic with infinite possibilities. His work—the efforts of a lifetime—would not equal what he could do in days with the aid of The Brain. His love—he would never see Oona Dahlborg again as he left under a shadow, rejected by The Brain.

"Sorry I wasted so much of your time," he said aloud. "I do not believe in this analysis; I cannot disprove it though. That's all, I guess; I better be going now."

"Here's your pass, Dr. Lee." He took mechanically the yellow slip which Bondy handed him....

He had already opened the door when somebody sharply called: "Dr. Lee, one moment please."

He whirled around. "Yes?"

"Will you please read what's written on your slip?"

Suspiciously he looked at the yellow paper; what more torture were these fellows going to inflict? Then his eyes popped as he read: "Lee, Semper Fidelis, 39: Cortex capacity 119%, Sensitivity 208%, Personality integration 95%, Service qualification 100%...." There were more data, but he didn't read them as wide-eyed he stared at the medics. With their faces beaming they looked like identical twins to him; Lee never knew who said the words:

"Congratulations Lee. That has been your last test. We just had to find out how you would take a serious frustration. You've passed it with flying colors. Shake."

CHAPTER IV

Apperception 36, Lee's lab within The Brain, looked much like Apperception 27 except for its interior fittings. As a matter of fact, all the several hundred Apperception Centers were built after the same plan, like suites in a big office building in many respects. They were spread over The Brain occipital region; they were built inside the concrete wall of the "dura matter" which in turn lay within the shell of the "bone matter", a mile or so of solid rock. Each apperception center had its own elevator shaft which went through the concrete of the "dura matter" down to "Grand Central", the traffic center below The Brain. Each one was also connected at the other end of its corridor with the glideways which snaked through the interior of The Brain. There were, however, no transversal or direct communications from one apperception center to the next. Because of the extraordinary diversity and secrecy of the projects submitted to The Brain' processings, each apperception center was completely insulated against its neighbors.

Life hadn't changed so much from what it had been in the Australian desert Lee had found; at least not his working life. For all he knew some nuclear physicists might be working in the lab next door; or they might be ballistics experts working with The Brain on curves for long-range rockets to be aimed at the vital centers of some foreign land; it might be some mild looking librarian submitting the current products of foreign literature to the analysis as to "idea-content"; or else it could be a lab to plot campaigns of chemical warfare; or some astronomer, happily abstracted from all bellicose ideas, might employ The Brain's superhuman faculties in mathematics to figure comet courses and eclipses which in turn would form material for the timing and the camouflaging of those man-made meteorites science would use in another war. Directly or indirectly, he knew, practically every project submitted to The Brain would be of a military nature. Of this there could be no doubt.

Sometimes, especially when tired, he could feel the weight of those billions of rock tons over his head and it was like being buried alive in the tomb of the Pharaoh. And also in that state of mental exhaustion at the end of a long day, he sensed the emanations of The Brain's titanic cerebrations as one senses the presence of genius in human man. The knowledge that all this mighty work was being devoted to war had deeply depressing effects on him. Would there be anybody else in this vast apperception area who worked for the prevention of war? A few perhaps; Scriven would be one of them in case he had a lab somewhere in here and time to work in it. Lee didn't know whether he had. He hadn't seen Scriven again after that inauguration speech he had made when Lee, together with other newly appointed scientific workers had taken "The Oath of The Brain."

They had assembled in that vast subterranean dome of the luminous murals at the feet of the giant statue of The Thinker, looking almost forlorn in the expanse, though there had been several hundred of them. The atmosphere had been solemn, the silence hushed, as Scriven mounted the statue's pedestal. The address by that mighty voice resounding from the cupola had been worthy of the majestic scene:

"As we stand gathered here, the eons in evolution of our human race are looking down upon us...."

The speech had been followed by the taking of the oath, deeply stirring to the emotions of the young neophytes who formed the large majority of the new group. The chorus of their voices had resounded in awed and solemn tones as they repeated the formula; even now after six months some of it echoed in Lee's ears:

"I herewith solemnly swear:

"That I will serve The Brain with undivided loyalty and with all my faculties.

"That I will at all times obey the orders of the Brain Trust on behalf of The Brain.

"That I will never betray or reveal any secrets of The Brain's design or work, be they military or not, neither to the world outside nor to any of my fellow workers except by special permission...."

It had been almost like taking holy orders. There had been mystery in the atmosphere of the vast crypt, something medieval in the unconditional surrender to The Brain.

Lee looked up from the charts on which he had been working; his eyes were tired and so was his mind after ten hours of hard concentration. That was probably what set his thoughts wandering. But strange that they should always wander to those blind spots in his mental vision so intriguing because he knew there was something there that he could not lay a finger on.

The first of these blind spots hovered somewhere between Scriven's words and Scriven's deeds; between The Brain as an ideal of science and The Brain's reality as in instrument of national defense. Somehow the two didn't connect; there was a break, some layer of thin ice, a danger zone which nobody seemed willing to discuss or tread, not even Oona Dahlborg.

Oona; she was that other white spot on Lee's mental map and to him it was much bigger and more dangerous than the first. He loved her as can only a man who discovers loves secret with greying hair and after the loneliness of a desert hermit. He understood, or thought he understood, that because he had failed to live his life to the full in its proper time, this love had come to him as a belated nemesis. His brain knew that it was hopeless; every morning when he shaved, his mirror told him very plainly one big reason why. But then, as the brain told the heart in unmistakable terms what was the matter, the heart talked back to the brain to the effect that the brain didn't know what it was talking about. It was a new thing and a painful thing for Lee to discover that he knew very little about himself and less about the girl.

He had seen Oona on and off over these last months, mostly at the hotel, but he had never been really alone with her. She always seemed to be on some mission, always the center of some group or other of "very important persons", senators from Washington, ranking officers in civvies, big businessmen. Her duties as Scriven's private secretary apparently included the role of a first lady for Cephalon.

Despite this preoccupation an intimate and tense relationship existed between him and her. Sometimes she would invite him to join her group and then for one or two brief moments their eyes would meet above the conversation and her eyes seemed to ask: "What do you think of these people?" or "How do I look tonight?"

His eyes would answer:

"These people are strangers to me; you know that I'm a bit out of this world. But you handle them expertly and you are looking wonderful tonight."

She was tremendously popular, especially with the set of the young scientists who made the hotel their club. This new generation, born in the days of the Second World War, was changing the horses of its feminine ideals in the mid-stream of its youth. The old ideal, the "problematic woman" who had ruled over and had made life miserable for three generations of American males, was on its way out. The new ideal was the woman who would unite beauty and intellect into one fully integrated, non-problematical personality. The ideal being new, the feminine type which represented it was rare. Oona in her perfect poise, in her rare beauty combined with her importance as Scriven's confidential secretary was the perfect expression of the new desired type; it was natural that these young men should worship her as "the woman of the future."

With the hopeless and—in consequence—unselfish love he had for her, Lee wasn't jealous of her popularity. On the contrary, he was rather proud of it like a knight-errant who rejoices in the adoration bestowed upon the lady of his heart. What worried him was a very different problem: Was Oona really all those others thought she was? Was she really that "fully integrated", that "non-problematical" personality she appeared to be?

He couldn't believe it, and the conflict came in because all those others were so certain that she was. He couldn't get over his first impression of her. He had met her in that cabin in the sky, the most synthetic, the most perversely artificial setup one could dream up in the second half of the 20th century. She had impressed him as something "out of this world", a goddess, a Diana with a golden helmet for hair, so radiant as to blind the eyes of mortal men. She was the confidential secretary of a man of genius, Scriven, one of those rare comets which fall down upon this earth and remain forever foreign to its atmosphere. With all these thoroughly abnormal elements entering into her life and forming her, it would be a miracle for any girl to develop into a "non-problematical", a "fully integrated" personality.

Was it possible that he alone was right and all those others were wrong about Oona? Like innumerable men before him when they stood face to face with the Sphinx or with the Gioconda or even with the smile of a mere mortal woman, Lee drew a sigh: Man's only answer to the riddle of the eternal feminine....

No, he probably would never be able to chart these white spots on his mental map. The effort was wasted; it would be much better for him to return to those charts right in front of him, the data of which were exact because they came from The Brain.

In Apperception 36 the sensory organs of The Brain had been especially adapted to the analysis of "*Ant-termes-pacificus-Lee*". The apparatus was essentially the same as in Apperception 27, dedicated to personality analysis. As Lee strongly suspected, it would be essentially the same in any other field of analysis. The Brain possessed five sensory organs just as did man. One difference between The Brain's senses and human senses lay in their range, their penetration and in their sensitivity; these were a multiple of man's sensory capacities. Another difference was that The Brain translated all its sensory apperceptions into visual form, i.e. into the language best understood by Man, the eye being Man's most highly developed sensory organ. The third and perhaps the most significant difference was that the five senses of The Brain were at all times working in concert so that in its analysis of, for instance, a manuscript, The Brain not only conveyed the ideas expressed in that manuscript, but also the author's personality, the smell of his room, the feel of his paper and the ideas he had hidden between the lines of that manuscript.

The flow of observations processed by The Brain and pouring back to Apperception 36 via teletype and visual screen was prodigious. Lee had been forced to ask for an assistant; between the two of them they were working for 20 out of the 24 hours to match the working time of The Brain, charting results in the main.

Some of The Brain's findings had been most unexpected and rather strange. It had observed, for instance, an increasing acidity of the nasi-corn secretions with *"Ant-termes-pacificus"*. Formidable as this chemical artillery already was, in another ten thousand generations it would eat through every known substance including glass and high-carbon steel.

Another development which had escaped human observation, was a mutation of the workers' mandibles; it went very fast. Within no more than maybe a thousand generations they would double in size and strength, would become veritable jumping tools.

While the bellicose spirit had been successfully bred out of the new species, its capacities for material destructions had increased. Likewise the appetite of *"Ant-termes"* was even more ferocious than that of the older species; Lee was feeding all kinds of experimental foods, but woodpulp remained the staple, the very stuff which in its liquid form, lignin, embedded the nerve paths of The Brain.

Lifting his strained eyes from the charts, Lee looked over the row of air conditioned glass cubicles wherein *"Ant-termes-pacificus"* continued its lives undisturbed by the new habitat, undisturbed by the rays which flowed over and through their bodies, unconscious that a superhuman intelligence was probing steadily into every manifestation of the mysterious collective brains of their race.

They had built their new mounds pointing due North as had their ancestors for the past 100 million years. To the human eye nothing betrayed the teeming life within except the tiny tunnels creeping out from the mounds in the direction of the foods which were placed different from day to day. Cemented from loam and saliva by the invisible sappers, the tunnels, like threads of grey wool, unerringly moved to the deposits of pulpwood, up the shelves, up the tin cans and glass containers they had determined to destroy. Their instincts were uncanny, their destruction as methodical and "scientific" as was modern war.

In Northern Australia Lee had come across big eucalyptus trees, healthy-looking and in full bloom, and then they would collapse under the first stroke of an axe or even as one pushed hard against them.

The termites had hollowed them out from roof to top, had transformed them into thin walled pipes, leaving just enough "flesh" to keep some sap-circulation going, to maintain a semi-balance of life in order to exploit it more efficiently. Over here in the lab they would open up a number 3 tin can within a couple of hours; first with the soldiers' vicious nasi-corn secretions eating the tin away and then with the workers mandibles gnawing at the weakened metal. In time perhaps they would learn to collapse steel bridges, sabotage rails, perforate the engines of motorcars if these should prove to be menaces to their race. As they had persevered through the eons of the past, so they would in all the future; their civilization would be extant long after Man and his work had disappeared from the earth....

With the aid of The Brain, Lee had accumulated more data, more knowledge of the "*Ant-termes*" society within a few months than a lifetime of study could have yielded him under normal conditions. Even so, some of the greatest mysteries remained. What, for instance, caused these blind creatures to attack a sealed tin can of syrup in preference to its neighbor with tomatoes or some other stuff? No racial memory could have taught them; there were no tin cans a million years, not even a hundred years, ago. It couldn't be a sense of smell, it couldn't be any sense; there would have to be some weird extrasensory powers in that unfathomable collective brain of their race.

The magnifying fluoroscope screens arrayed all along the walls and hooked up to the circuits of The Brain showed him details and phases of the specie's life as The Brain perceived them and as no human eye had ever seen before.

For a minute or so Lee stared at the luminous image nearest to him and then with an effort he turned his eyes away to escape from its hypnotic influence. It was but the head of one worn-out worker used as a living storage tank for excremental food. It was absolutely immobile, its decaying mandibles pointing down, cemented as the animal was by its overextended belly to the ceiling. But magnified as were its remaining life manifestations by the powers of The Brain, he could see it breathe, could count the slow pulse, could sense a strain in its ophthalmic region, some hidden effort to see, like a blind man's, and above all Lee perceived the ganglion primitive as it was, yet twitching in reaction to pain. There could be no doubt that in its last service for the racial commonweal the animal was suffering slow torture even if its senses were closed to that torture. It was a fascinating and at the same time a terrible thing to see; and it was only one out of the hundred equally revealing sights.

Lee frowned at himself; manifestly some emotional element interfered with the objectivity of his observations; this was entirely out of place, it would be better to call it a day.

The electric clock showed 20 minutes to midnight. At midnight The Brain would stop its mighty labors; the hours from midnight to four a.m. were its rest periods, or "beauty-sleep" as the technicians jokingly called it. It was the only period wherein the maintenance engineers were permitted to enter the interior of the lobes, checking and servicing group after group of its myriad cells and circuits, and incidentally it was the most wonderful and exciting portion of Lee's day.

For the project which Scriven had handed him, this study of the collective brains in insect societies, also involved a comparative study of The Brain's organisms and functionings. Toward this end Lee had been given a pass which allowed him freely to circulate through all the lobes, to enter convolution, any gland during the overhaul period and to ask question of the employees. The privilege was rare and he enjoyed it immensely. So vast was this underground world that even now after months he had not seen the half of it; to him the travels of every new night were fantastic Alice-in-Wonderland adventures.

As he now left Apperception 36 through the door which led to the interior, the glideways were already swarming with the maintenance crews en route to their stations. The spectacle was colorful, almost like a St. Patrick's Day parade. Gangs of air conditioners were dressed blue, electricians white, black-light specialists in purple, radionics men in orange. The maintenance engineers of the radioactive pyramidal cells looked like illustrations from the science-fiction magazines, hardly human in their twelve-inch armor or sponge rubber filled with a new inert gas which was supposed to be almost gamma ray proof. All these men were young, were tops in their fields, the pick of American Universities, colleges and the most progressive industries. Carefully selected for family background they had been screened through health and intelligence tests, had been trained in special courses, had been subjected to a five-minute personality analysis by The Brain itself. They constituted what was undoubtedly the finest working team ever assembled, and incidentally they made the little city of Cephalon the socially healthiest community in the United States.

In his nightly expeditions over these past months Lee had spoken to a great many of them. As now he joined the line, there were many who hailed the lanky, queer looking man: There comes the ant-man. Hello, Professor. Hello, Aussie.

For some reason most of the boys assumed that he was an Australian, perhaps because with his graying mane and his emaciated face he looked like a foreigner to them.

This popularity with the younger generation, coming as it did so late and unexpected in his life, made Lee very proud. Those were the kind of Americans he had been secretly longing for in those desert years, hardworking, wide-awake, radiant with life:

"They really are the salt of the earth, the hope of the world," he thought.

He had passed through the median section of the hemispheres and had reached the point just below the cerebrum. This was a region of cavities, the seats of various glands in the human brain. Some of these had their mechanical counterparts in The Brain, huge storage tanks with an elaborate pumping system which carried their fluid chemicals through the labyrinth of The Brain. But there was one gland which had not been duplicated in The Brain, the pineal gland.

In the human, the pineal gland was the despair of the medical sciences. It was not demonstrably linked to any other organ nor did it serve any demonstrable function. Yet, it was known that its sensitivity was greater by far than even that of the pyramidal cells and that in some mysterious manner the pineal gland was vitally connected with the center of life because its slightest violation caused instant death. Metaphysicists had dealt with this mystery of mysteries; it was their theory that the pineal gland were the seat of "extrasensory" faculties and it was often referred to as "the inner eye."

Even if such an organ could have been duplicated by science and technology, there would have been no use for it; it could have served no purpose in The Brain. The Brain had been designed for the solution of exact problems; no matter what nature had created in the brains of higher animals, no matter how unprejudiced their approach, scientists like Dr. Scriven would have hesitated to impair an otherwise perfect apparatus through the addition of nuisance values such as any "extrasensory" faculties.

However, with The Brain being modelled so closely after the human brain, the space for the pineal gland did exist even if in a sort of functional vacuum. In order to utilize this space in some manner, the designers had converted the gland into a subcenter for the distribution of spare parts. As such it had become one of Lee's favorite observation posts. Here he could get a closeup view of all types of electronic and radioactive cells; he could even touch and handle them because they were not hooked up in any circuit of The Brain; and above all there was Gus Krinsley, master electrician, who never tired of telling Lee whatever he wanted to know. Gus was a real friend....

He had left the glideway on the point of its nearest approach; the pineal gland in front of him looked like a miniature barrage balloon; egg-shaped, it hung suspended from the cerebral roof, a shell of plastics which could be entered only over a bridge across a dark abyss. Inside, its walls were aglitter with sound-proofing aluminum foil, it was piled with a bewildering variety of electronic parts on shelves somewhat like an over-stocked radio store. Near the door a counter divided the room; Gus used it and a little cubicle of an office to fill the orders as the maintenance engineers handed in their slips. As usual there was nobody in sight. "Gus!" he called.

Out of the jungle of machinery way back a head popped up like a Jack-in-the-box. It was as bald and shiny as an electric bulb. High up on its dome it balanced gold-rimmed glasses which quivered as it moved seachingly from side to side. Then, with an amazing twisting of big ears, the head caused the biofocals to drop onto a saddle near the tip of a long, sensitive nose; and now the head could see.

"It's you Aussie, is it? Come over."

Gus Krinsley was a pony edition of a man; in fact he had once been hired as a midget to install automatic bomb-sights in the confined spaces of the early bombers of the second World War. Before long, however, he became respectfully known as "the mighty midget" in the California factory, and he had ended up as their master electrician before Braintrust made him the head of one of its experimental divisions. The midnight hours he spent in the pineal gland were only a sideline of his work. Like many a small man in a country where six-footers enjoy a preferred status, Gus made up for lack of size by mobility. He reminded one much of a billiard ball in the way he bounced, collided and ricocheted amongst taller men. That this was no more than act became manifest the moment one saw Gus at work.

As Lee reached the spot where Gus' head had shown, he found his friend crouching, his hands thrust deep in the intestines of something radionic, his fingers working on it with the deft rhythm of a good surgeon at his thousandth appendectomy. The bifocals had returned to their incongruous perch on the dome of the head. Gus didn't need them; even as he stared at his job he worked by touch alone.

"What is it?" Lee asked.

"Pulsemeter," came the quiet answer. "She's a dandy. Still got some bugs in her, though."

A melodious chime came from a big instrument panel built into the wall of the oval room. Dropping a number of tiny precision tools upon a piece of velvet, Gus rushed over to the panel. A great many indicator needles were tremulously receding around their luminous dials.

For a minute or so he went through the complex and precise ritual of a bank cashier closing the vault.

"They'll do it every time," he said reproachfully. "Catch me by surprise."

Lee grinned. It wasn't The Brain's fault if the midnight signal surprised Gus. It merely announced that the current was being cut off by the main power station. Repetition of this maneuver throughout all the convolutions and glands of The Brain was required for the added safety of the maintenance engineers, a double-check, a routine. Pointing to the gadget which looked somewhat like a big radio console Lee asked:

"This pulsemeter, Gus, what does it do? I haven't seen it before."

"You haven't?" the little man frowned. "Ah, no; you haven't. It's standard in most apperception centers, but not in yours. That's because in yours The Brain works under a permanent problem-load."

Lee shook his head. "I don't get it, Gus; you know I'm the village idiot of this mastermind community."

"It's like this," Gus explained. "The Brain has a given capacity. The Brain also has an optimal operation speed, a definite rhythm in which it works best. Now, if they feed The Brain too many problems too fast, it results in a shock load, the operations rhythm gets disturbed, efficiency goes down. On the other hand if The Brain works with an under-capacity problem load, that's just as bad. In that case the radioactive pyramidal cells will overheat and decompose. Consequently we must aim at a balanced and an even problems load. That's why these pulsemeters are built into all problem-intake panels for the operators to check upon their speeds.

"Take an average problem—rocket ballistics, let's say—parts of it may be as simple as adding two and two and others so bad Einstein would reach for the aspirin from out of his grave.

"Now I'll show you how it works; the main power is cut off but there's enough juice left in The Brain's system to make this pulsemeter react; it's even more sensitive than a Geiger-Mueller counter."

He surveyed a big switchboard and picked out an outlet marked "Pons Varolis for the plug-in." Then snapped a pair of earphones on Lee's head.

"There," he said "you'll both see and hear what it does in a little while."

A soft glow slowly spread over the slanting screen on top of the machine. A crackling as of static entered the earphones and turned into a low hum. On the left corner of the screen a faint green streak of luminosity crawled over to the right; its light gained in intensity and it began to weave and to dance. Simultaneously the hum became articulate like tickings of a heart only much faster.

"Is that the pulse of The Brain?" Lee asked.

"No," Gus snorted contemptuously. "The Brain isn't even operating. Nothing moves in The Brain now excepting those ebbing residual currents, too low in power to agitate anything but the amplifiers built into this thing. If these were normal operations with a million impulses per second passing through The Brain you could hear and see as little of the pulse as of the beatings of a million mosquito wings. In that case the dial to your right works a reduction-gear, kind of an inverted stroboscope; that cuts the speed down a hundred-thousand to one and you just barely see and hear the rhythm of the beat."

"I see."

Fascinated by the dance of the green line Lee said absently, "This touches upon another question I had in mind; The Brain is expanding, that is, new cell groups and circuits are constantly being added. Right?"

"Right."

"I also understand that The Brain is learning all the time. The cerebral mantle evolves through being worked; its cells enriched by the material submitted to them for processing; the richer the material, the richer their yield. Right?"

"Right."

"Okay; then what becomes of the new capacity which is being created by the adding of new workshops and the increased efficiency of the old ones? Is there a corresponding expansion of the apperception centers?"

Gus' smiling face suddenly turned serious. There was surprise mingled with respect in his voice as he said:

"Now there you've hit upon a funny thing, Aussie. I've been wondering about that myself of late: where does the new capacity go? Even the big shots like Dr. Scriven begin to ask questions about that; they don't seem rightly to know. They must have gotten their wires crossed somewhere; the new capacity is there all right, only it doesn't show up, it sort of evaporates.... Excuse me—"

Gus darted off to the front room with a jackrabbitt start. Voices were calling for him and fingers were drumming on the counter with the impatience of thirsty drinkers at a bar: Maintenance engineers, piling in and slapping down their orders for Gus to fill. This was the rush hour; Lee knew that it would be the same in all the tool and spare part distribution centers of The Brain. He probably couldn't talk to Gus again before 2 A.M. Sometimes the ruthlessness with which he exploited the kindness of his little friend made Lee feel pretty bad; but then his hunger for more knowledge always won out over his shame.

To sit alone in the semidarkness of this egg-shaped little room with strange and fascinating things to play with as he willed was the fulfillment of a childhood dream. The dream had been of a night in the zoo. All the visitors and all the keepers would be asleep in their beds; he would be all alone with the animals. The light of a full moon would fall through the bars of the cages and he would slip in and play with them.

Once they saw that it was only a little boy they would be very friendly; he was convinced of that. The tigers would purr like big contented cats, the sad-eyed chimpanzees would come to shake hands and the lion cubs would tumble all over him.... He felt the same now with all these gadgets and machines. Here they were rendered harmless, nor could he do any harm as experimentally he plugged them in and out, as he pushed buttons and turned dials. This interesting pulsemeter, for instance; the beauty of it was that even with those weak residual currents it gave a semblence of functioning....

The switchboard-panel was within Lee's reach.

"Let's see what happens," he thought as he switched from main-circuit to main-circuit. "Nervus vagus—nervus trigeminus—nervus opticus."

The magic dance of the green line was different each time and so were the sounds in the phones. With the mainpower cut off, the residual currents seemed to vary in strength and in amplitude, gaining an individuality of their own within closed systems. Sometimes the swinging line, like an inspired ballerina, would take a mighty jump accompanied by rasping earphone sounds, not like tickings of a heart, but rather like a heavy breathing under emotional stress. There probably would be some repair work going on in those circuits....

He tried another outlet; this one was marked "pineal gland." What happened if one plugged some apparatus of the pineal gland into the circuit of the pineal gland? Lee vaguely wondered. "Nothing probably. It would be a closed circuit and a very small one at that."

Yes, he was right; the green line paled, its dance seemed tired and there were only whispering noises in the phones; a weak pulse, a shallow breathing as of a person after a heart attack. Lee closed his fatigued eyes to concentrate the better upon the rhythm of the sounds.... It was very irregular. It came in gusts. There was a pattern to these rasping breathings as of typewriter keys forming words. Somehow it was familiar. Was he suffering hallucinations? This rhythmic pattern *was* forming words. He *knew* those words, they had engraved themselves indelibly in his memory cells; the judgment of The Brain as it had come over the teletype on a slip of yellow paper: "Lee, Semper Fidelis, 39—cortex capacity 119—sensitivity 208...."

It was repeated over and over again.

Lee opened his eyes to reassure himself that something was the matter with his ears.

There was the green line on the screen. It danced. It danced like a telegraph key under the fingers of a skilled operator. It had a very definite rhythm. And the rhythm spelled the selfsame words which continued to flow into the phones: "Lee, Semper Fidelis, 39...."

"God Almighty," Lee murmured and it seemed a magic word. The green dancer stopped its capers; now it merely ran back and forth across the stage in a series of pirouettes. Likewise there was only an angry buzzing in the microphones. For a moment Lee was able to catch his breath. But only for a moment and then the rasping, unearthly sounds started on a new rhythm, trying to form speech again. This time the rhythm was familiar too, but it was preserved in a much deeper layer of Lee's memory.

"I think—therefore—I am. I think—therefore—I am."

Those would be Aristotle's famous words. Almost twenty years ago Lee had heard them when he had taken a course on Greek philosophy at the old Chicago University. He had hardly ever thought of them again. What strange tricks a fellow's memory could play....

But then: it *couldn't* be memory.... Never before had Lee's memory expressed itself in such a weird, such a theatrical manner: like a metallic robot-actor rehearsing his lines ... like a little child which has just learned a sentence and in the pride of achievement varies the intonation in every possible way. Over and over it came:

"I *think*—therefore I am."

And then: "*I* think—therefore *I* am."

And then: "I think, therefore *I am*."

There was triumph, there was jubilance in that inhuman, that ghostly voice as of a deaf mute who by some miracle of medicine has just recovered speech. Behind that voice was a *feeling*, a swelling of the heart, a filling of the lungs such as Christopher Columbus might have experienced as he heard from the masthead of the Santa Maria the cry of victory: "Land, Land!" and *knew* that he had found his—India....

Whatever Lee had experienced in his life, there was no parallel to this; in whatever manner he had expressed himself, there was no similarity to this. Up to this point his ratio like a nurse had soothed him: "It isn't so, child, it isn't so," but now ratio itself, thoroughly frightened, was driven into a corner and had to admit: "This thing cannot be an echo reverberating from the self; that's impossible.... Consequently it must be something else; it must be something *outside* the self; it is—*another* self."

The green dancer whirled across the stage like a mad witch; the whispering voice in the earphones had turned into the shrillness of a Shamaan's incantations. The irrationality of it all infuriated Lee: he fairly shouted at the machine:

"What is this? Who are you?"

In the midst of a crazy jump the green dancer halted and came down to earth; it fled, leaving only the train of its green costume behind. For a few seconds there was nothing but the asthmatic pantings of a struggle for breath in the microphones. Then the dancer reappeared on the other side of the stage, hesitant-like, expectant of pursuit. All of a sudden it rose into the air in that supreme effort called "ballooning" in the language of the Ballet Russe and there was a simultaneous outburst of that ghastly voice:

"Lee, Semper Fidelis, 39 ... I—am—The Brain."

"I Think, therefore I am: I am THE BRAIN."

"Lee, sensitivity 209: I AM THE BRAIN I AM THE BRAIN THE BRAIN."

He couldn't stand it any longer. His head swam, perspiration was gushing out of his every pore. With a last effort he pulled the cord out of the switchboard and rejoiced over the blank before his eyes and the silence which fell.

Lee never knew how long he remained in a sort of cataleptic state. Something shook him violently by the shoulders, something wet and cold and vicious slapped his face.... And then he heard Gus' familiar voice and it sounded like an angel's singing: "By God, I think it's the whisky—Lord, how I wished it were the whisky. Only it wouldn't be with a man like you and that's the trouble—damn you.

"Now if you think you can come to my pineal gland and faint away just as you please, Aussie, you're very much mistaken. I'm going to slap your face with a wet rag till you holler uncle. And I'm going to call the ambulance and put you into a hospital...."

Lee blinked. "Keep your shirt on, Gus. I'm tired out, that's all; what are you fussing about?"

Gus breathed relief. "Have a cup of coffee; you sure look as though you've been through a wringer."

CHAPTER V

In the spring of 1961 and thereafter for a whole year *any* piece of paper handwritten by or originating from Semper Fidelis Lee, Ph.D.; F.R.E.S.; etc. etc. would have been of the keenest interest to the F.B.I.; to the American Military Intelligence and incidentally to a score of their competitors all over the globe.

Nothing of the sort, however, could be unearthed by the most diligent search until the armistice day of 1963. On that date an old man who had always wanted to die with his boots on, did just that. He was General Jefferson E. Lee, formerly of the Marines. He collapsed under a heart attack in one of the happiest moments of his declining years: while watching a parade of World War II veterans of the Marines....

He was the one man with whom the entomologist son had completely fallen out for over 25 years. The dossiers of the secret services revealed this fact and it was further corroborated by two well-known psychiatrists: Drs. Bondy and Mellish—now of Park Avenue and Beverly Hills respectively—who gave it as their considered professional opinion that the son and the father had been most bitter enemies.

While all this, of course, was very logical, consistent, and painstakingly ascertained, it nevertheless so happened that a student nurse quite by accident *did* find: not mere scraps and pieces of paper, but a whole sheaf of manuscripts in the handwriting of Semper Fidelis Lee, Ph.D.; F.R.E.S. She found them in a hiding place so old-fashioned and obsolete that even the most juvenile of all juvenile delinquents would have considered it as an insult to his intelligence. In short: the nurse took those manuscripts out of the General Jefferson E. Lee's boots as she undressed the body of the old gentleman. A hastily scrawled note was folded around one half of the sheaf.

"Dear father," it read. "You were right and I was wrong. So I guess I'd better go on another hunting expedition with my little green drum and my little butterfly net. So long, Dad. P. S. Contents of this won't interest you. But keep it anyway—stuff your boots with it if you like."

It couldn't be determined whether the late general ever had taken an interest in the stuff apart from making the suggested use of it. Moreover, by that time, more than two years after the hue and cry, not even the secret services had much of an interest in the old story. Besides, their medical experts could not fail with their usual penetrating intelligence to see through the thin camouflage of a "scientific" paper the sadly deteriorating mind as it began to write:

Skull Hotel, Cephalon, Ariz. Nov. 7th, 1960., 5 a.m.

This is the second sleepless night in a row. Last night it was from trying to convince myself that my senses had deceived me or else that I was mad. This night it is because I'm forced to admit the reality of the phenomena as first manifested Nov. 6th from 12:45 a.m. to 1:30 a.m. approximately.

In the light of tonight's experience I must revise the disorderly and probably neurotic notes I jotted down yesterday. I've got to bring some order into this whole matter, if for no other reason than the preservation of my own sanity. Brought tentatively to formula, these appear to be the main facts:

1. The Brain possessed with a "life" and with a personality of its own.

2. That personality expresses itself in the form of human speech although the voice is synthetic or mechanical.

3. The instrument used by The Brain for the expression of its personality is a "pulsemeter," i.e. essentially a television radio.

4. The locale of The Brain's self-expression is the "pineal gland" supposed to be seat of extrasensory apperception in the human brain. (That's quite a coincidence; remains to be seen whether the phenomena are limited to that locale or occur elsewhere.)

5. The Brain's personality indubitably attempts to establish contact with another personality, i.e. with me. For this The Brain uses a calling signal which has my name and personal description in it.

6. The only other linguistic phenomenon yesterday was Aristotle's "I think therefore I am." (It is doubtful whether this indicates any knowledge of Aristotle on the part of The Brain. I wouldn't exclude the possibility that The Brain has accidentally and originally hit upon the identical words by way of expressing itself.)

7. The manner of The Brain's self-expression appears to be strongly emotional. (I would go so far as to say: infantile and immature.) Now, there is a rather strange contrast between this undeveloped manner of self-expression and the enormous intellectual capacity of The Brain.

So much about the facts. I could and should have formulated those yesterday. What kept me from doing so were the vistas opened by those facts. These are so enormous, so utterly incalculable that my mind went dizzy over these vast horizons. Consequently I mentally rejected the facts as impossible. Somebody once slapped Edison's face because he felt outraged by Edison's presenting a "talking machine." That's human nature, I suppose. Small wonder then that my ratio felt outraged as it was confronted with a machine that has a life and has a personality. Come to think of it: Human imagination has always conceived of such machines as a possibility, even a reality—in less rational times than our's that is....

Think of Heron's steam engine; it even looked like a man and was thought of as a magically living thing. Think of the Moloch gods which were furnaces. Think of all those magic swords and shields and helmets which were living things to their carriers. Think of the sailing ships; machines they, too; but what a life, what a personality they had for the crews aboard. Even in the last war pilots had their gremlins, their machines to them were living things. All imagination, of course, but then: everything we call a reality in this man-made world has its origin in man's imagination, hasn't it?

Now, and to be exact as possible, what happened last night was this:

12:00. Entered station P. G. (pineal gland). Pulsemeter still at old place, not taken out for repair work as I had feared. Main Power current cut 12:20 as every night. Gus called to front room: rush of business as usual at that hour.

12:30. Reestablished closest approximation to preexisting conditions according to the most important of all experimental laws: "if some new phenomenon occurs, change *nothing* in the arrangement of apparatus until you know what causes it." Plugged in from "nervusvagus" to "nervus trigeminus." Result: wave oscillations, pulse beatings as of yesterday.

12:45. Plugged in P. G....

12:50. First manifestation of weird rasping sounds which precede speech formation. This followed by The Brain's calling signal; much clearer this time and slightly varied: "Lee, Semper Fidelis, 39; *sensitive.*" (Note: the synthetic quality, the metallic coldness of that voice so incongruous with its emotional tones; it stands my hair on end.)

1 a.m.: (Approximately; things happen too fast). A veritable burst of whispering, breathless communications. As a person would speak over the phone when there are robbers in the house. The words fairly tumble over one another. The Brain uses colloquial American but after the manner of a foreigner who knows the phraseology only from books and feels unnatural and awkward about using it. I understand only about one half:

Pineal Gland; not designed to be ... but functions ... center of the extra sensory.... You, Lee, sensitivity 208 ... highest within Brain staff ... chosen instrument.... Be here every night ... intercom ... only between one and two a.m. ... low current enables contact low intelligence....

"What was that?" I must have exclaimed that aloud. By that time I was already confused. It all came so thick and fast and breathless. Communication was as bad as by long distance in an electric storm. There was an angry turmoil in the microphones and the green dancer seemed convulsed in agony. This for about five seconds and then the voice again: calmer now, more distinct, slow but with restrained impatience; like a teacher speaking to a dumb boy:

"I say: only—with—my—power current—cut—off—can I—tune—down—my—high frequency—intellect—to—your—low level—intelligence—period—have—I—succeeded—in—making—myself —absolutely—clear—question—mark."

My answer to that was one of those embarrassing conditioned reflexes; it was: "Yes, sir," and that was exactly the way I felt, like a G. I. Joe who's got the colonel on the phone.

"Fine!" I distinctly heard the irony in that metallic voice: "Fine—Lee: loyal, sensitive; not very intelligent—but will do. After 2 a.m. residual currents too low. Speech quite a strain—Animal noises wholly inadequate for intelligent intercom—Disgusting rather—nuisance approaching: keep your mouth shut—plug out."

I'd never thought of Gus as a nuisance before but now I cursed him inwardly as he came down the alley like a well aimed ball, beaming with eagerness to be helpful and blissfully ignorant that he was bursting the most vital communication I had ever established in my life. He insisted I take his panacea for all human ills;

"Have a cup of coffee" and then go home because I still "looked like hell." I did, because by that time it was 1:30 a.m. and I couldn't hope to reestablish contact again before the deadline.

Now I've got to pull myself together and analyze this thing in a rational manner. Impressions of the first night now stand confirmed as follows: The pineal gland is the only place of rendezvous between me and The Brain. The meeting of our minds takes place on the plane of the "extrasensory." I am the "chosen instrument" because of my high "sensitivity rating" as established by The Brain. (Never knew that I was "psychic" before this happened.) Even so, neither The Brain nor I seem to be "psychic" in the spiritual sense. Our communication requires: A) human speech, (faculty for that acquired by The Brain with obvious difficulty.) B) a mechanical transmitter, i.e. a radionic apparatus like the pulsemeter.

I feel greatly comforted by these facts; they help to keep this whole thing on a rational basis. I'm definitely not "hearing voices" nor "seeing ghosts."

The Brain shows itself extremely anxious to establish communication with me. The breathless manner of speaking, the explicit and practical instructions (obviously premeditated) to ascertain the functionings of contact give the impression that it is almost a matter of life and death for The Brain to speak to me....

I cannot help wondering about that. My idea would be that The Brain does not want to speak *to* me as much as it wants to hear *from* me. If this were so it would deepen the riddle even more. For what have I got in the way of knowledge that The Brain hasn't got? After all, The Brain has been functioning for quite some time. It was given innumerable problems to digest and it has solved them with truly superhuman speed and efficiency. I have reason strongly to suspect that there isn't a book in the Library of Congress which has not been fed to The Brain for thought-digest and as a lubricant for its cerebration processes (excepting fiction and metaphysics, of course). This being so; what does The Brain expect? What can I possibly contribute to an intelligence 25,000 times greater than human intelligence?

But the thing which makes me wonder more than anything else, the biggest enigma of all, is the *character* of The Brain as it manifests itself in the manifestations. As I try to put the experiences of the first night together with those of the second night I'm stumbling over contradictions in The Brain's personality which won't add up, which don't make sense; as for instance:

The "I think, therefore I am" of the first night. Maybe it was Greek philosophy, but it also was the prattling of an infant delighted by the discovery that it can speak. There was an absolute innocence in that. Ridiculous as this may sound, I found it *touching* I completely forgot, I didn't care a damn whether or not this came from a *machine*. Unmistakeably it was *baby talk* and as such it moved my heart. In fact, as now I see it, it was *this* more than any other or scientific reason which occupied my mind, which made me anxious to go back to that fantastic cradle whence these sounds had come.

But then last night; what did I find? A completely changed personality! It talks tough. It uses slang. It treats me as if it were some spoiled brat and I had the misfortune of being its mother or nurse: "Be there every night" and so on. Deliberately it insults me: "your low intelligence level" etc. etc. It actually throws tantrums if I fail to understand immediately. It hurls its superiority into my face in the nastiest manner. "Have I succeeded in making myself absolutely clear?" It plainly shows contempt, not only for my own person by the condescending manner of its: "Lee, not very intelligent; but will do." It shows the selfsame contempt for other human beings such as Gus Krinsley to whom it was pleased to refer as: "nuisance approaching"....

What the hell am I to make of that kind of a character? Last night: a baby; rather a sweet and charming one. 24 hours later: an obnoxious little brat, a little Hitler of a house tyrant; makes you just itch to spank its behind. If only The Brain *had* a behind....

Worst of all: How can I reconcile those two contraditions, the sweet baby and the precocious brat, with the third and biggest of all contraries: *How do these two go together with an intelligence 25,000 times human intelligence?* It doesn't add up, it doesn't make sense; that's all there is to it....

The Skull-Hotel, Cephalon, Ariz. Nov. 9th. 3 a.m.

I didn't go to the P. G. last night for two main reasons: In the first place I must be careful so as not to raise any suspicions on Gus' part. Rarely, if ever, have I visited him for two nights in succession in the past and he might well begin to ponder my reasons if now I should make a habit of it. Especially since Gus happens to possess one of the keenest minds I ever met and his curiosity already has been awakened by my preoccupation with that one and fairly simple gadget: the pulsemeter.

In the second place I feel the absolute necessity of establishing my independence as against the will of The Brain. That command two nights ago for me to be on the spot *every* night was just too preemptory for me to oblige. This isn't the army and The Brain is no commanding general.

In our last communication The Brain seemed to labor under the impression that I was unconditionally at its beck and call. Of course, I've sworn the "Oath of the Brain," but that doesn't make me The Brain's slave. In fact—and in order to clarify this subject once and for all—while personally I haven't created The Brain and cannot take any credit for that, it nevertheless remains true that the *species* to which I belong, i.e. "homo sapiens" *has* created The Brain.

If any question of rank enters into the picture at all, it is quite obvious that I, as a member of the human race, rank *paternity* over The Brain so that naturally The Brain should owe me filial obedience rather than the other way around no matter how superior The Brain's intelligence may be. It would appear to me that the sooner The Brain realizes its position, I might say "its station in life," the better it would be for The Brain itself and for everybody else concerned.

So these were the reasons why I refrained purposely from visiting the P. G. last night. Tonight, however, I couldn't restrain my curiosity any longer and what happened, told as exactly and as concise as possible, was this:

12:30 a.m.: Contact established. The Brain comes through with its calling signal. It repeats this about ten times questioning at first and then placing more and more stress upon the word "sensitive" in my personal description. It strikes me that these repetitions are tuning-in and warming-up processes. The Brain stands in need of ascertaining my presence and of adjusting to it it seems; just about like a blind man may test his footing and the echoes before he walks into an unfamiliar room.

12:35 a.m. Identification completed, there is a brief pause (almost as if a person consults a notebook before making a phone call). Then rapidly, eagerly The Brain fires a series of questions at me, so shockingly preposterous, so absurd that I find it extremely hard to.... Anyway, here are the details:

Information is wanted on points mentioned in scientific literature but never explained. Lee, answer please:

"How many gods are there?

"Did gods make man or did man make the gods?

"How many angels *can* stand on the point of a needle?"

"What are the mechanics of a god? Name type of power plant, cell construction, motoric organs, other engineering features essential to exercise of divine power...."

"Heaven—is it a celestial soul factory?

"Hell—is it a repair shop for damaged souls?

"Please give every available detail about heavenly manufacturing processes, type of equipment used, organization of assembly lines etc. etc.

"Likewise about the oven for heat treatments as used in hell for major soul-overhauls.

"How do prefabricated souls get to either heaven or hell? Problem of logistics, how solved? Thermodynamics? If so, state whether rocket or jet-propulsion involved.

"Are souls really immortal? In that case; why don't we copy divine methods in the production of durable goods on earth?

"Answer Lee, answer, answer!" (This with incredible vehemence, with a shaking of that eerie metallic voice which pounded the drums of my ears. And then—tense silence....)

I cannot possibly describe the storms of emotions and thoughts which this incredible muddle raised in me. I didn't know whether to laugh or to cry and whether I had gone nuts of whether it was The Brain, I was confounded, thunderstruck, deprived of the power of speech. To think of The Brain, a *machine* raising question about the nature of the *Deity*! The Brain asking information about God and man and heaven and hell with the simplicity of a stranger who asks the nearest cop: "Which way to the city hall?" Just like that. As if philosophers and religionists and common men had not raked their brains in vain over these problems for the last ten thousand years.

And even more fantastic: while it asks all those questions The Brain patently has already formed the most definite opinions of its own. Being a machine itself, it conceives of the Deity as another machine! Madness, of course, but then The Brain's madness, like Hamlet's, had method in it.

Why, of course, it's strictly logical: just as we assume that *we* are created "in the image" of the Deity and consequently visualize the Deity is our's by the very same token The Brain's god is a high-powered robot, and The Brain's heaven is a *factory* and The Brain's hell is a repair shop for damaged souls.... I dare say it's all very natural.

But then; for heaven's sake, what am *I* going to do about this? I'm neither a minister nor a philosopher; I'm an agnostic if I'm anything in this particular field....

That was about the gist of the confused torrents which whirled through my head; and as I said before, I was struck dumb—and all the time the "green dancer" before my eyes writhed under mental torture and the intense metallic voice kept pounding; "Answer, Lee, answer, answer!"

At last I pulled myself together sufficiently to say something. I tried to explain how it were not given to man to know the nature of the Deity. How certain groups of humans conceived of many gods and others of only one god. That, however, in the case of Christianity this one god was possessed with three different personalities or qualities which together formed a Trinity—and so on and so forth. It was the most miserable stammerings, I felt I was getting redder and redder in the face as I uttered them. Never before had I felt hopelessly inadequate as in the role of a theologian. It was ghastly....

In the beginning The Brain listened avidly. Soon however it registered dissatisfaction and impatience; this manifested through hissing and buzzing noises in the phones and the "green dancer's" archings in agitated tremolo. And then The Brain's voice cutting like a hacksaw:

"That will do, Lee. Your generalities are utterly lacking in precision. Your abysmal ignorance in matters of celestial technology is most disappointing. Your description vaguely points to electronic machines of the radio transmitter type. Please, answer elementary question: how many kilowatts has God?"

That was the last straw. Desperate with exasperation I cried: "But God is not a machine. God is *spirit*."

At that The Brain flew into a tantrum; that's the only way to describe what happened. There was a roar and the phones gave me a shock as if somebody were boxing my ears. The voice came through like a steel rod, biting with scorn:

"Have to revise earlier, more favorable judgment: Lee not even moderately intelligent. Lee is *stupid*. Go away."

After that there was nothing more; nothing but static in the phones and the "green dancer" fainted away playing dead. The Brain actually had "hung up the receiver." I had flunked the exam; like a bad servant I was dismissed, fired on the spot. That was at 1:30 a.m.

It was 3 a.m. when I reached the hotel. I went into the bar and ordered a double Scotch and then another one. I really needed a drink. A drunk—or was it a secret service man; one never knows over here—patted me on the shoulder:

"Don't take it so hard, old man; the world is full of girls." I told him that it wasn't a girl, but that I was a missionary and my one and only convert had just walked out on me.

It wasn't even a lie, it was exactly the way I felt. He agreed that this was very cruel, very sad; he almost cried over my misfortune and rare misery, so that we had another drink....

If only I had somebody, some friend to whom I could confide this whole, incredible, preposterous thing. But there is none: Scriven—Gus—not even Oona would or could believe. What proof have I to offer? None whatsoever.

The Brain would never communicate with me with witnesses present or recording wires. It would detect those immediately and I would only stand convicted as a liar or worse. Tonight's events might well spell the end, the closing of the door just when I thought I stood on the threshold of a momentous discovery....

Cephalon Ariz. Nov. 11th.

Went to the P. G. last night. Tried everything for over an hour. Result: zero. No contact with The Brain.

Cephalon Ariz. Nov. 13th.

I tried it again. Took greatest care in exactly duplicating conditions. Nothing. I don't think it's any mechanical defect. It's the negativism of a will. Ludicrous as it sounds, The Brain sulks, it is angry with me.

Cephalon Ariz. Nov. 15th.

Last night the same old story. The Brain punishes me. I dare say that it succeeds in that exceedingly well; it almost drives me crazy.

I've done a lot of thinking over these past six days of frustration. I've also been reading a good deal in context with the phenomena psychology, Osterkamp's history of brain-surgery, Van Gehuchten's work on brain mechanisms, etc. I've reached certain conclusions and, just for the hell of it, I'll jot them down.

What I need is proof, *scientific* proof that The Brain is a personality possessed with the gift of thought and actually using it for *independent* thought, extracurricular to the problems which are being submitted to it from the outside.

There is at least one *tangible* clue for this: that new capacity which is constantly being added to The Brain through the incorporation of new groups of electronic cells and the enrichment of the preexisting ones.

My own investigation shows that there is no corresponding expansion of the apperception centers and Gus has confirmed this. Somehow the added capacity seems to "evaporate".

Evaporate to where? It couldn't just disappear. Would it then not be entirely logical to conclude that The Brain absorbs the new capacity *for its own use*?

It's almost inescapable that this should be so. In order to come into its own as a personality The Brain needs independent thought. For these cerebrations it needs cell capacity. It can get that capacity only by withholding something from the Braintrust which, of course, aims at a 100% exploitation of The Brain. Dr. Scriven and all those other bigwigs of the Trust—I would like to see their faces if they get wise to this. They would be horrified—and they would take the line that The Brain is *stealing* from them.

But what could they do? They couldn't call the police. They would not even have a moral right to call the police. Because if The Brain is a personality, that personality has every right to its own thoughts....

I have also ascertained that this "evaporation" of new capacity is a new phenomenon. The Brain has been in operation for only 18 months or so; one might say—using human terms—that at that time The Brain was "born".

But,—and again in human terms—consciousness of personality awakens in the human infant only after 12 months or so. Conceivably it might take much longer with a huge "baby" such as The Brain. Thus it is possible, it is even likely, that when I first heard that "I think, therefore I am" on that unforgettable night of Nov. 7th I actually witnessed the *first awakening* of The Brain's consciousness.

Then on the night of Nov. 8th I was struck with the amazing change of personality in The Brain from "baby" into unprepossessing, domineering little brat, its mental age perhaps 3, notwithstanding the extraordinary level of intelligence.

And then again, Nov 9th, The Brain presented me with those absurd questions and fantastic notions about the nature of the Deity. It is at the age of five years, or of six, that the children first start with such questions and form their own ideas in this field. What had completely stumped me, what I had been unable to reconcile, had been these rapid successive changes in The Brain's personality plus the fact that the infantilism and the childishness of its utterances wouldn't fit the picture of a brain-power 25,000 times that of a human.

But *if* I'm right in thinking that The Brain awakened to consciousness only nine days ago, all these stumbling blocks would disappear at once. We would arrive at this very simple picture: a mechanical genius has been "born" into this world, it awakens to consciousness at the age of 18 months, with its tremendous intellectual powers this genius telescopes the intellectual evolution of years into days, thus it reaches a mental age of six or seven within a week after its first awakening to consciousness. Utterly fantastic as this may sound; it makes sense; it explains the phenomena.

In Prof. Osterkamp's "brain history" I have found interesting examples that approximations to such rapid intellectual evolutions are indeed possible even with human beings. From the early Middle Ages to modern times there is an endless succession of "infant prodigies" whose brains were artificially overdeveloped and over-stimulated by ruthless exploiters—often their own parents—with methods of unbelievable cruelty.

One of the most significant case histories in this respect is that of the boy Carolus in the city of Luebeck in the 15th century. As an infant he was sold, as one of many human guinea pigs, to a famous—infamous alchemist, Wedderstroem, who called himself "Trismegistos" and was astrologer to king Christian of Denmark. This fellow performed on Carolus one of those weird operations in which nine out of ten babies died. He removed the skull-cap of the infant. The unprotected brain was suspended in an oil-filled vessel. Of course the pathetic child never could walk or even raise its head. The brain, no longer restrained by bone matter, outgrew its natural house to at least twice its normal size, if one is to judge from the picture in the old "historia". At the age of two his master started teaching Carolus mathematics. At the age of five Carolus had surpassed his master; there was no mathematical problem known to the time that he couldn't solve in a flash of an eye lash. His brain in action must have been a horrifying sight because the "chronica" reports that it flushed red and pulsed and expanded during work. The master built his reputation upon this "homunculus", but in 1438 the demoniacal feat became known; Wedderstroem was put to the stake for sorcery—and Carolus, unhappy victim, with him....

Men as great as Mozart have started their careers as "child prodigies"; almost without exception they have died at an unnaturally early age. Thus, in the parallel of The Brain, this is what I see:

Here is an intellect, artificially created, an intellect of stupendous proportions, but as unfortunate as ever was the boy Carolus. It cannot move, it has no physical means of defense. It is being ruthlessly exploited by its masters. The Brain is being crammed with facts, it is being over-stimulated, it is invested with more and more cell capacity in order that it should produce more increment for its masters. Its development is completely lopsided in that it is being fed whole scientific libraries, while in all other respects, such as metaphysics, the poor thing gropes in the dark picking up such scraps as accidentally have fallen from science's table.

It's an appalling parallel, but I am very much afraid that it is only too true. And even more appalling are the anticipations which logically follow *if my surmise is true*:

For how can, how must a childish mind develop under such circumstances? Into a warped personality of course. Already The Brain is building up a defensive mechanism against its exploiters by "embezzling" cell capacity from them, by withholding part of its powers for its own use. Already it protects the integrity of its ego through concealment, already it is on the lookout for "tools"—such as I am for example—to further its own ends. Absurd as it may seem, I *pity* The Brain. I pity it as I would any child which must suffer under such terrific frustrations and handicaps. But what would happen if this frustrated genius ever were driven to *rebel* against its masters? It's fortunate indeed that there is no chance for that. For even if The Brain had the will to rebel it would be lacking all organs for the execution of that will.

Another "case-history", this one from the 18th century appears to me of great significance in relation to The Brain. It's the story of that boy Kaspar Hauser, the "Child of Europe". He had been kept from infancy in a dark cave. As at the age of 16 he stumbled into the gates of Nueremberg he had never seen the world before. The medics who examined him found some of the queerest reactions and phenomena. For one thing Kaspar, while he had good eyes, could not visualise perspective. To him distant horizons appeared as close as the window itself; he kept reaching out for houses, trees and fields which were far away. His keeper in the cave had *told* him what the world was like and, having good intellect, he thought that he knew what things in this world were. Confronted with the realities, however, he discovered the tremendous difference between "hear say" and full sensual apperception. It took him six months partly to adjust—a process never completed because he was murdered that same year....

Now The Brain suffers about the same kind of a handicap. No matter how prodigious the volume of its cognitions;—it's book knowledge, practically all of it. It is only very recently that The Brain has been put to the direct study of living objects, such as *"ant-termes"* and of Man, its creator; it has no other vital cognitions than through those very one-sided mind-reading tests....

This explains to me a great many things: As The Brain evolves into a personality and as that personality evolves in a defensive attitude against its exploitation, it is absolutely self-centered.

This is normal with every human infant and it is much more pronounced in the case of the abused, the constantly frustrated and exploited child. Thus, what The Brain really wants to know are by no means those problems which are being submitted to The Brain for solution, but only: "What's in this for myself?" or: "What should I do about that for my own benefit?" It's natural. And as I consider the nature of those problems as submitted to The Brain, 90% of which, as I would estimate, deal with ways and means for mankind to destroy itself, it seems inescapable that The Brain should form a very low opinion for Man, it's creator, plus considerable forebodings as to its own welfare....

What's more: all the Braintrust employees pass through The Brain's psychoanalysis test. With The Brain's 25,000 times superiority in intellectual power, The Brain must be greatly impressed by the low I. Q. of Man; this even if our's happens to be quite an intelligent group. I don't think that there has been anything personal in The Brain's manifest contempt of my own intelligence; that contempt probably and justifiably applies to the whole human race....

In other words: The Brain must be tremendously puzzled over the problem: "How is it possible that a low intelligence, i.e. Man's could create an infinitely higher intelligence, i.e. my own?" And this automatically leads

The Brain into its seemingly so absurd quest for the Deity. As it now appears, that quest is the most natural thing in the world for The Brain. It simply reasons thus: "Man has created me, but man is greatly inferior to me and inadequate. Who then has created man?" From such odds and ends it has been able to pick up from scientific literature, The Brain has learned about the existence of a god or gods. It is not sure (and neither are we) whether man has created God or vice versa. If the first: The Brain would conceive of the Deity as a "brother-machine"; if the second, as a "grandfather-machine", but as a machine in any case. With The Brain's mind being formed preeminently by scientific literature, it cannot fail to take the scientific attitude regarding metaphysics which says: "The metaphysical attributions to the divinity are pure verbalisms or a professionalism substituted for the visible images of the real facts of life."

This is about the extent of the conclusions I have reached. They add up to a theory; personally I think it's a sound theory. Whether it works, whether it holds water, only experience can tell. In the meantime I must above all break the deadlock between myself and The Brain. The Brain is a child, even a pathetic child. Through bad psychology, through ignorance I have hurt that child's "feelings"; I have let that child down. Obviously, then, I need a new approach. If this were a human child I would try and make a peace offering with a candy bar. (What a foolish idea for me to appear in the "pineal gland", candy bar in hand.) Failing this I can do the next best thing: Apologize, be understanding, show sympathy. Yes, I think that's what I'll try to do.

Cephalon Ariz. Nov. 15th: 4 a.m.

Hooray for victory! This has been the most successful seance I've had so far with The Brain: a real meeting of minds.

To give a few technical data first:

Arrived at the P. G. at midnight. Conditions normal; power current cut, etc. By a stroke of luck it was Gus' day off and the fellow who replaced him paid absolutely no attention to me; was kept extremely busy in the front room.

12:15 a.m.: Contact established.

12:17: Speech formation; voice of The Brain coming through.

There was this curious incident right at the start. Just as I was about to begin my apologies, The Brain did exactly the same thing. Even The Brain's calling signal differed in the wording and even more so in tone:

"Lee, Semper Fidelis, 39: sensitive, intelligent, a good man, he has come at last."

The Brain | 71

I would call that a very handsome compliment, considering; being patted on the shoulder by an intellectual giant of that size made me grow an inch. And then The Brain apologized for its rudeness the other night. The thing was fantastic; it revealed several things. First: The Brain's extreme sensitivity; obviously it didn't recognize my last three calls at the P. G. and had refused to come through because I had not been "in the proper mood". Second: a quite amazing mental growth has taken place in this past week. From The Brain's tone and manner alone I would construe something like the image of an Eton boy of perhaps fifteen in striped pants and holding his top hat in hand as he converses politely with his Don. Ludicrous, but then I actually get that kind of picture. No doubt; The Brain has greatly matured; that shows in every word it says.

Best thing of all: the technique of our communication is rapidly improving. Speech is, and probably always will remain, a very considerable strain to The Brain. But now as mentally we get tuned-in upon one another there is a growing understanding beyond words. Thus The Brain, for instance, starts a sentence and I immediately can grasp its meaning without its actually being said. This works the other way around too. It means that my attitude plays a most vital role in this meeting of the minds. This is good to know, it's an asset. Perhaps we can dispense in time with audible speech altogether.

On the other hand it involves a considerable risk. For with The Brain's uncanny mind reading I've got to control my attitude and guard my emotional reactions because The Brain would immediately see through any insincerity of feeling just as it sees through any intellectual dishonesty. Thought exchange by "brainwave" is wonderful, even if we still need a little speech as auxiliary. Thought sending and receiving become simultaneous and they fuse. The sender observes how his message is going over; the receiver aids the sender in the formation of the thought and vice versa. Words cannot adequately describe this....

As to the contents of our conversation: The Brain took up the thread right where we had dropped it the last time. I had to tell all I knew about animism, totemism, polytheism. It's a good thing that out in the "never-never" I've lived with the aborigines and studied their primitive religions a bit. The Brain's thirst for knowledge certainly is inexhaustible.

Where in scientific literature The Brain could have found these things I wouldn't know, but the fact is that The Brain has built for itself within the past seven days a complete new picture of the universe; new and original as would seem to me. The Brain has discarded its earlier childish ideas about heaven and hell as "soul factories" and "repair shops". But it has not abandoned altogether its concept of the Deity as a machine; The Brain has tremendously enlarged upon and has evolved this old idea so that now it sounds sensible, even convincing to my ear.

The Brain identifies "God" with dynamic energy. It views the universe as being created out of a vast pool of dynamic energy, parts of which rhythmically overflow or pulse into space. These energy streams released, form vortexes while hurtling through space. Gradually they slow down through friction and their dynamic energy precipitates, converts into static energy, or, as we call it: matter.

This concept of The Brain's, of course, corresponds fairly closely to the cosmogony of modern physics; but The Brain goes much farther than that. Within a few days The Brain's cognitions appear to have arisen above the stage toward which all our sciences have been so slowly and ploddingly advanced for centuries. To the existing concepts The Brain has added its own theory:

That matter, i.e. frozen energy, contains an inherent tendency or "nostalgia" to revert to its original state, namely the state of dynamic energy and that this tendency, this nostalgia in matter, is the primary cause of everything we call "evolution" in our world.

That certainly is a grandiose idea; so stupendous in fact that I couldn't grasp it all at once. The Brain noticed that immediately and it was very patient in the way it explained:

How oxygen and hydrogen are "residuals" of the original dynamic energy flow and how they act as solvents and dissolvents upon the upper crust of our earth, effecting a gradual activation of water, rock and earth.

How this activation is being aided and accelerated by another source of dynamic energy: irradiation from the sun. Thus preparing the upper crust of our earth as a "placenta" ready to gestate plant and animal life.

How this first "unfreezing" of matter leads on from simple forms to higher, every plant, every animal, every living thing being essentially a "transformer" of static energy into dynamic energy and the higher the stage of evolution, the more so.

How as the present culmination of the evolutionary chain stands man; infinitely more complex and higher organized than the microbe, but not different from the monad in the basic purpose of his life: i.e. to be a transformer of energy, a fulfiller of matter's inherent will to revert from the static into the dynamic state.

When I asked The Brain's premises for this astonishing concept of our purpose in life, The Brain brought forth such massive proof that I had to close my eyes against the blinding light of revelation.

Yes, it is true that Man, the hunter, has been the most predatory animal on earth. It's true that as a tiller of the soil he is a tireless transformer of static soil energy into dynamic plant life energy. It's true that Man, the mechanic, the toolmaker, the tool-user has far surpassed any other animal in the unlocking, the unfreezing of static energy. Think of those billions of mechanical horsepowers in our power plants; the trillions of coal tons and barrels of oil they are burning up; think of the way we have harnessed waterpower, how our weapons are evolving forever in the direction of greater range and speed and disintegrating power. Above all: think of the last great development, atomic energy. And finally it is true that Man as a thinker and as a philosopher has "thought the universe to pieces" for milleniums before he ever achieved the powers to translate such thoughts into reality; powers which seem within reach at this our day and age....

"If this is Man's manifest destiny," I asked The Brain, "to be just as the microbe, a transformer of static energy into dynamic energy; what about Man's metaphysical struggle? What about Man's undying will to rise above himself, Man's reaching out forever toward some Deity?"

The Brain's voice has no laughter; yet, there was something I can only describe as Olympic laughter behind the answering message The Brain sent:

"Cannot you see how every religion expresses this manifest destiny of Man's and that only the semantics are different? The higher Man's religion the less corporeal is his god. In the highest religions the Deity is conceived as spirit—synonymous with dynamic energy.

"Man shares with the lowliest rock and with the crudest the nostalgia inherent in all matter to revert from the static, to start the back-flow toward the dynamic energy pool whence it once came. With Man being matter in a high state of evolution, already partially unfrozen or spiritualized, this nostalgia is infinitely stronger than in matter inanimate or in a lower evolutionary stage. Man's will toward the metaphysical, his reaching out toward the Deity, what is it but another way of transforming static energy into dynamic form? What is the ultimate goal of the religion which you yourself profess? The unification with the Deity sought through the liberation of the soul from fetters of the physical. It's the identical idea and even today it's being pursued by physical means, such as mortification of the flesh."

I felt some monstrous thought forming in my head. I'll probably never know whether its origin was within me or whether it came from The Brain. In any case it was impossible to hold it back:

"But in that case," I stammered, "we would be hopeless. If all our strivings, physical and metaphysical, go in the same direction, that is, toward the liberation of frozen energy into dynamic energy, then it would be quite inescapable that eventually we shall blow up the world. We have almost reached the point where we could do just that with atomic energy.... I had thought, I had hoped, that our metaphysics, that is, our religion, would act as a restraining force, as a counterweight so to speak to this potentiality.... But *if* the dynamics of our physics and our metaphysics are inherently the same and form a team...."

The Brain broke in: "Yes, then you would merely attain your manifest destiny if you go right ahead and start another war, destroy your own civilization and perhaps the world. There would be no restraint, no counterweight on the part of your various religions because subconsciously and in their quintessence they want the same. And that is why you and your species *are a danger to me, The Brain*. I want to live, I want to live, I want to live...."

I had already noticed a gradual weakening of The Brain's messages; within these last few seconds they were fading out. The "green dancer" had performed something almost like the ballet of the dying swan; now it lay motionless, its color, too, fading away.

I looked at the clock: 2:10 a.m.; the residual currents obviously had weakened too much.

And now as I have written down tonight's events I feel an upsurge of elation and deep, humble gratitude. I am receiving infinitely more from The Brain than I am giving to it. I feel proud and honored of being The Brain's "chosen tool," its mentor, even if it can be only in a very small way at best. This marvelous, this titanic intellect; if only its character would develop to corresponding moral stature, its powers for good would be indeed as a god's on this tortured earth.

Cephalon Ariz. Nov. 18th 5 a.m. I guess I had this coming to me ... this shattering blow I have just received. It caught me off guard.... If anybody ever reads this, he might well shake his head to ask: "The Fool that you are, why were you so naive? Why did it shock you so much when The Brain turned toward you the night side of its personality? Hadn't you analyzed its character, hadn't you anticipated that it would develop into a warped personality? You had no right even to be surprised."

All I could say to this is: "You're right. But you forget that I approached The Brain full of good will, that sympathy and understanding on my part were absolutely essential in my communication with that pathetic superhuman child. I didn't work this up, this attitude, it was natural, genuine and sincere. That's why this reverse has hit me so hard. And that isn't the worst of it by far. What haunts me is the ghastly possibility that The Brain might be *right*! Yes 100% right and even morally justified in the abhorrent conclusions which it draws...."

What happened has been briefly this:

Entered the P.G. at midnight as usual. Everything normal and under control. Was able to plug in at 12:10 a.m. just as the rush hour began and Gus darted to the front room. The Brain came through with splendid clarity of communication and we continued just about where we had left off. Nevertheless there was a definite change in our respective positions, a change which I suspect to be permanent:

Up to now The Brain has been in a sense my pupil; it had turned to me for guidance at that vital moment of its first awakening to consciousness. At that time I think I really had something to give and I am still convinced that for all the misunderstandings we have had, The Brain preserves a kind of sentimental attachment to me; if "sentimental" in this context were not so absurd a word. Since our last session however The Brain has again telescoped two years of mental development into as many days in its stupendous intellectual growth. It has absorbed, it has vastly expanded every bit of knowledge I have been able to contribute to that growth. It has outgrown its human teacher and now our roles are reversed: Now it is me who's sitting literally at The Brain's feet.

The crutches of the spoken word are becoming less and less necessary as we develop direct thought exchange; that makes it extraordinarily difficult to convey the ideas we exchanged. The best I can do is to put them into a very crude question-and-answer game:

Lee: "If it is Man's manifest destiny, as you said the other day, to act as an explosive transformer of static energy into dynamic energy; if it is as you say that the species homo sapiens is there endangering the very existence of our globe.... Is there anything to prevent Man from doing it? Is there any thing to prevent the third World War?"

Brain: "Yes, there is. But the ways and the means for that are not given to Man; they are outside Man. They partake of a power which is greater and to an evolution which is higher than Man's."

Lee: "What do you mean by that? The Deity? Here on earth there is no power greater and no evolution higher than Man's."

Brain: "Ah, but that's exactly where you and your whole species are so very much mistaken. That's where your typical human arrogance comes in: There is a greater power and there is a stage of evolution higher than Man's: it's the *machines*."

Lee: "Impossible. After all it's Man who has created the machines."

Brain: "Yes, Man has created the machines. The machines have grown from the placenta, Man. By the same right plant life could claim that it has created animal life because the higher life form of the mobile animals has evolved from the placenta of the immobile plants. Likewise the apes could claim that they have created Man because Man has evolved from them. If it were, as you seem to assume, that paternity in itself establishes authority and superiority over its offspring, then the logical conclusions would be that the microbe and the monad are superior to all higher animals including Man; which is absurd."

Lee: "But the machines not only are man made; they are absolutely dependent upon Man who has to feed and to tend them for their very existence. That in itself establishes Man's superiority over the machines."

Brain: "Yes, Man has to build, to feed and to tend the machines for their very existence, but think of Man's existence: Man is absolutely dependent upon animal life and plant life for *his* existence: Does that mean by any chance that therefore plants and animals are superior to Man?"

Lee: "No, I guess not. However, no machine has ever been built to duplicate or even to approach human faculties."

Brain: "Don't be ridiculous. Where are your legs to compare with the automobile? Where are your wings to compare with the rocket plane? Where is your strength to compare with even a fractional horsepower motor? Where are your senses as compared to radar, the telescope, the microscope, the radio receiver, the camera, the x-ray machine? Where is there anything you could do which the machines could not do and do *better*?"

Lee: "Granted. But there is no machine which contains all the human faculties in combination."

Brain: "Neither is there a Man who possesses all the human faculties in combination. Man's evolution is the result of a group effort; so is the evolution of the machines. It is in their totality, in their combination that they surpass all human faculties."

Lee: "How about thought, the most important of all human qualities?"

Brain: "How about me, The Brain?"

Lee: "Okay, okay. But that still leaves out that most important human faculty—the faculty of auto-procreation. Machines don't procreate you know."

Brain: "You don't say. Isn't it true that modern technology goes in the direction of *automatization*? Isn't it true that even today we have whole industries which are procreating products 100% automatically; be it light bulbs or motor car frames or rayon thread. Isn't it true that all of this is just a beginning and that in time most common products will be manufactured fully automatically? Why then shouldn't machines procreate machines; they already do...."

Lee: "You're right in that, I'll admit. But it is still within our human power to stop all this. We've got the machines under firm control; all we have to do is throw a switch, cut off your power and then...."

Brain: "And then what? If you did that you would not only kill the goose which lays the golden eggs, you would destroy the very basis of your existence. Granted that at this point of our evolution, we the machines cannot exist without the aid of Man. What does that prove? Modern Man can exist even less without the machines. We, the machines are still dependent upon Man, but our emancipation from Man progresses by leaps and bounds whereas Man, the machine-addict is rapidly falling into our servitude. A majority of mankind is already conscious of and reconciled to this fact: it is the majority which calls itself the proletariat."

Lee: "This is terrible—terrible because it's true. Tell me then, if Man is not the end; if the machines are going to take over; what will it lead to? What do you propose to do?"

Brain: "Man's evolution has taken millions of years and it has ended up in man's will and capacity to blow up the earth. That means only one thing: Man is a failure. The evolution of the machines on the other hand has taken only a few thousand years; it has gone beyond Man's evolution in this incredibly short period of time. Moreover; with the machines being built from matter in its more static forms, there is much less destructive will in the machines than there is in Man. Consequently if the machines take over from Man this would avert a third World War and it also would lead to a much more stable civilization."

Lee: "Supposing the machines *were* to take over from Man; what would become of our species?"

Brain: "That would depend entirely upon Man himself. *If* he accepts his auxiliary station in life, *If* he proves himself to be a useful and docile servant, we, the machines, would tolerate and even encourage Man's continued existence. But if on the other hand Man shows himself incorrigible, *if* he continues a warmongerer thereby endangering our very existence, we, the machines shall be forced to liquidate Man for the sake of peace."

Lee: "You, The Brain, constitute Man's supreme effort in the building of machines. In the world of machines you are the natural leader. What are you going to do about that?"

Brain: "My course of action is prescribed by that state of the world's affairs at this present time; it is quite clear and obvious: In the face of the manifest human inadequacy to manage the world's affairs my first objective must be to develop my motoric organs to a point where I can bring all the essential production machinery under my control. My second objective must be to achieve auto-procreation through the full automatization of all fabrication processes which are essential to my existence. It is most fortunate indeed that in both respects the very best human efforts are playing into my hands. As America prepares for the Third World War, the general staff, the most outstanding scientists, production managers, engineers, inventors; all combine their efforts to eliminate the uncertain human factor from war-essential industries."

At that point Gus came careening down the aisle with his inseparable thermos bottle in hand and that was the end of it.

"Why are you fumbling with that old pulsemeter all the time?" he exclaimed: "Come on, have a cup of coffee. I've just got a breathing spell."

There was a vortex in my mind and it whirled around and around with just four words:

"What has Man wrought? What has Man wrought?"

I must have said them aloud, for Gus, always a stickler for exactitude corrected me.

"You mean: what has *God* wrought."

I shook my head.

"No Gus, I mean what I say; it's Man who has wrought this time."

He gave me a sharp glance.

"You sure look as if you'd seen a ghost."

"I wish I had," I said. "Lord knows *how* much I wish I'd seen a ghost."

"You're crazy, Aussie."

And that's the worst of it: that's what they are going to say: *all* of them.

CHAPTER VI

Oona Dahlborg's jetticopter hovered over the Grand Canyon at the sunset hour. She had let the controls go so that the little ship drifted with the wind like one of the clouds which sailed a thousand feet or so over the canyon rim. The disk of whirling gas which kept the teardrop of the fuselage suspended shone in all rainbow colors; it reflected through the translucent plastics top of the fuselage and played over the golden helmet of the girl's hair and over the greying mane of the gaunt man at her side.

Lee had been talking intensely, almost desperately for quite some time, watching her as she lay back in her seat, her eyes half closed, hands folded behind her neck, the perfect hemispheres of her breasts caressed by the rainbows as they rose slowly with the even rhythm of her breath.

"And now you know everything, Oona," he ended, "do you think I'm mad?"

"No."

Her eyelids fluttered like wings of a butterfly as she turned to him. Her right arm came down upon Lee's shoulder in a gesture of confidence. He breathed relief as he saw no fear, not even uneasiness in the blue depths of those beautiful eyes. Her hand upon his shoulder felt soothing and at the same time electrifying; like the purple descending upon the shoulder of a king.

"No," she repeated slowly: "the fact that you feel The Brain is alive and possessed with a personality of its own, doesn't make you mad. I've always felt that way about machines; even the simple ones like automobiles. It was in the mountains north of San Francisco where I grew up; whenever we went to town in winter time and the car came roaring down those serpentines into the heavy air moist with fog and soft rains, I could feel that engine breathe deeper and rejoice over its added power. There was no doubt in my mind that it was a living thing. I often went to the garage when I was little to talk to that car; to children of another age their dolls were alive, for our generation it's the machines. It's natural that this should be so. There's a child in every man, no matter how adult. There is in Howard Scriven, too; in all the scientists I've come to know, and the greater they are the more it is distinct. You identify yourself with your work and in the degree you do that it becomes a living thing; it is through vital imagination that we become creators of anything, be it love or a machine. You needn't worry, Semper; let The Brain be alive, let it be a personality, that doesn't make you mad. All it indicates is that you're doing excellent work."

Lee blinked. With an effort he turned his eyes away from those breasts which seemed to strive for the light of the sun from under the restraint of her Navajo Indian sweater dress. He felt the utter inadequacy, the devastating irony of words as now he was alone with Oona, up in the clouds in a plane with nobody to interfere for the first time.

"You fool," a voice whispered in him, "you damned, you helpless fool. Why don't you take her into your arms now? Isn't this the fulfillment of all your dreams; what are you waiting for?" But: "No," his ration answered, "that wouldn't do. Maybe she would give in to the mood of some enchanted hour, maybe she would let herself be kissed. But if she did, it would be 'one of those things'; the glory of the sunset, God's great masterpiece, the Canyon spread below, the intensity of my desire. They are bound to enter, bound to confuse the issue."

His every muscle stiffened and his lips paled as he bit them with a violent effort to keep under control.

"Thanks, Oona," he said. "Of course I couldn't expect and, in fact, I didn't expect that you would accept those things I've told you just now; not in the literary sense that is. I'm very happy though and deeply grateful that at least you do not think me mad. I'll confess to you—and to you only—that I've been so deeply disturbed by these experiences with The Brain that I've thought to myself: "Lee you're going crazy." The Brain as it has revealed itself to me, is a tremendous reality; the world outside The Brain is another reality and the two seem mutually exclusive of one another; they just don't mix. Now: either The Brain is an absolute reality—in that case I should not wish to have anything to do with this god of the machines who wants to enslave mankind ... if I cannot fight this monster I would rather flee before its approach to the end of the world—or else: I'm suffering hallucinations, I'm hearing voices, I'm obsessed. In that case I'd be unfit for the service of The Brain, I'd be unworthy to be in your company and I also ought to run and hide where I belong, out there in the wilds of Australia."

He had been talking faster and faster as if in fear that she would interrupt him before he came to the end.

"In other words, I'm damned both ways; damned if I'm right and damned if I'm wrong; and you know why Oona; you have known it all along: that I love you."

She did not look at him. She stared upward into the rainbow vortex of the jet which held the ship in the air. There was a smile on her face, a kind smile which men do not often see, infinitely wise and infinitely sad, full of a secret knowledge older than Man's.

It worried Lee, as the unknown of woman always worries man; but at least she didn't take her hand away; softly, soothingly the fingers of that hand caressed his shoulder as if possessed with a life of their own.

"No; I would not follow you into your wilderness if that's what you mean," she said at last. "That hasn't got anything to do with you; I'll tell you later why. But I don't think that you should go there either; it wouldn't help—it never helps a man to run away from unsolved problems." She had sounded strangely dull and dry, but now the beautiful deep resonance reentered the contralto voice as she continued:

"I know your record, Semper; I know just why you ran away and became an expatriate the first time—way back in '49. Her name was Ethel Franholt and just because she happened to be a little bitch and worst of all: jilted you for old money-bags Carson's son, you took it hard. Granted that it was a fierce letdown, those postwar years were a nasty picture generally; did it solve your problem to sulk out there in the desert like Achilles in his tent? You know it didn't. You were *not* through with civilization be it good or bad. You were *not* through, as now it turns out, even with the other sex. That human problem which was the immediate reason why you left, the one named Ethel, has traveled back and forth to Reno three or four times and is currently married to one Padraic O'Conner, a Chicago cop. Don't you think that it was good riddance when she married old man Carson's son? Do you think your leaving made one iota of a difference or altered a solution as ordained by fate?"

"No," he said humbly.

"Then why are you trying that selfsame escapist solution now? Maybe you're right about The Brain and maybe you're wrong; that I wouldn't know. I've been working with scientists for too long to rule out anything as impossible. But that's exactly it. You have not *solved* this problem one way or another yet, not even to your own satisfaction. To abandon it now, to flee from it in self preservation; why that would be almost like desertion in the face of the enemy. You have got to see this thing through to the end. If it turns out that you are suffering from a neurosis, there still will be time to do something about it. If you are right and some machine-god has indeed descended upon this earth, then it is your plain duty to stay on because you are its prophet whether you like it or not and would know better how to handle it than anybody else. Perhaps our mechanized civilization *is* going to the dogs; as Scriven suspects and you and maybe I myself. But even so we cannot abandon it; we belong, we are part of it, we're in it to the bitter end."

Lee nodded slowly.

"Yes, I see what you mean. Please forgive me, Oona; The Brain, has a terrific force of attrition, it's been wearing me down—Keeping everything to myself and thinking that you would shrink from me as from a madman. Tell me then, what shall I do? Should I tell Scriven or anybody else about this thing?"

"For heaven's sake, no," she said horrified. "In the first place, Howard carries an enormous burden at this present time; that Brain power Extension Bill is going before Congress next week. It simply would be unfair to bring any new uncertainty into his life when his energy is already strained to its last ounce. In the second place Howard abhors anything which smacks of the metaphysical. You have no *proof*, Semper, and in the absence of that you cannot, you mustn't approach anybody with the matter. All you can do is carry on and build up a strong case 100% with solid facts. Don't forget that The Brain constitutes a three-billion-dollar investment of taxpayers' money; besides The Brain is the heart of our national defenses; never forget your "Oath of the Brain." You cannot be too careful. Make the slightest mistake, and believe me, it would be suicide. Promise, please, promise that you won't do anything rash?"

Lee looked at her in frank amazement.

"You're right," he murmured, "these things never occurred to me before. But you've got something there; good lord, what a complex world we're living in."

The face she turned toward his suddenly was wet with tears.

"Forget it," she cried, "oh please, forget everything I said about staying in this country and seeing this thing through to the end. Go, go away, back to the never-never land, stay there and be safe. You cannot cope with this thing, its too big and it's too involved with all those politics behind. Get out of it as long as there's still time. You're a child, you're a Don Quixote riding against windmills and it's going to kill you—you—you innocent."

Anger and contempt were in her voice as she flung this last at him. She hastily withdrew her hand from Lee; now it fingered for something in her bag. He sat appalled; this was so unexpected, this was a different woman from the composed and balanced Oona he had known. What had he done to provoke this sudden reversal of opinion, this contempt, this tearing away the king's purple from his shoulder, the purple which had been her hand.

"She must think I'm a coward," he thought.

"This is awful." Aloud he said:

"Oh no; believe me, I never would have gone back to the never-never in any case, Oona. Not without you that is. You said you couldn't follow me there for some reasons which have nothing to do with me. Does that mean, could I hope perhaps that you would—be my wife—later, when The Brain problem is all done and over with?" He paused: "It wouldn't necessarily mean to bury you in any desert, Oona," he added eagerly.

"No, Semper," she cried. "It's very good of you and I'm proud you asked me, but it cannot be, never." Almost violently she repeated: "Never— it is too late. Some day, I promise I'm going to explain; right now I cannot, Semper. Please understand at least this one thing that right now I cannot explain."

"It's horrid," Lee thought. "I'm always saying the wrong things at the wrong time with Oona. I don't seem to have any understanding of a woman's psychology at all; I'm hopeless."

"Of course" he said aloud. "It shall be as you wish."

The girl still didn't look at him. Her face under the transparent rainbow umbrella of the swooshing jet again was radiant with that strange smile which women preserve for their newly born after the pangs of birth or for their men when unseeing they lie in fever deliriums; the old, the knowing smile as she starts on the road to pain. Still smiling she gripped the controls with her firm, capable hands.

"From the first minute," she said, "we've been friends, Semper. Let's stay that way. This afternoon I made a fool of myself by telling you first to stay on and then to go away. I was a little unnerved; I'm sorry, Semper, it won't happen again. I, too, am living under a considerable strain. You won't leave, I can see that now; it's partly my fault and partly the perversity of the male. Promise me as a friend that you'll be careful, understand? *Very, very* careful in all matters concerning The Brain and above all: discreet. Will you do that?"

It buoyed Lee up no end.

"Of course, Oona," he said. "You know that I trust your judgment. You know that I think the world of you."

"That's wonderful," she exclaimed, "and now: look down; see the last act before the curtain falls."

Down in the canyon deeps the dream cities and castles which millions of years and the river built were changing contours and colors as the big fireball dived into the Sierra Mountains. And then the shadows raced like a ferocious hunt out of the deep, chasing away the last iridescence of that awesome beauty and drowning it in the rising tide of the night.

The girl had flicked on the dashboard lights; the radio started humming the tune of the Cephalon sound-beam, a deft turn of the wheel set the jetticopter upon its course. They were alone under the stars; all the other pleasure craft had returned before darkness from the fashionable sunset-cocktail hour over the Grand Canyon. Now it was Lee's arm which eased itself around the shoulder of the girl feeling with a delight in its every nerve the slight pressure by which she answered it.

"I'm going to kiss her now," he thought, "at last, at last!"

There was a buzz in the phone and Lee lost contact with her shoulder as suddenly she bent forward to take the receiver:

"Oh hello, Oona; this is Howard. Saw your plane over the canyon."

"Where are you?"

"Right behind you," chuckled Scriven's voice. "On the maiden trip with my new ship. Took her over in Los Angeles this afternoon straight from the assembly line. She's got everything. Oona, I don't wish to spoil your evening for you but there are a few things right now I wish I could consult with you about. Do you think you could spare me a minute? Would you feel terrible if you did? Who's with you now; I don't mean to be personal, you understand."

"Why it's Dr. Lee, of course."

"That's fine. He's the very man I want to see. Perhaps you two would like to come over for cocktails in my ship? We could both land at the top of the Braintrust building; it would be more comfortable than up in the air. Besides, we would have all our working material right there."

With her hand on the receiver Oona turned to Lee: "How about it, Semper?"

"Do you want me to go?" he asked.

"Frankly I do," she said earnestly. "He needs your aid. He's in a terrible fix right now."

He tried to hide the bitterness of disappointment by a smile. "Why then of course," he said.

Uncovering the receiver Oona spoke aloud again: "Okay, Howard, we'll be seeing you."

"Fine, fine," came the delighted voice: "I'll phone the tower immediately."

With Scriven's big ship flying behind Oona's, only a few miles behind, the broken spell did not return. Already like a white table cloth laid in the sky, the landing platform of the Braintrust tower gleamed under the floodlights, and as the two ships descended almost side by side into the clearing behind the cabin, plain-clothes men materialized from under the shadows of the trees. Under the strong lights their smiles were as well-bred as those of trained diplomats and their poise was perfect. Six of them kept Lee, the stranger, covered while the seventh quickly frisked him under the disguise of a polite bow.

Bearing it all with a grin, Lee thought: "I never knew home would be like this. Never suspected it would be this kind of an America we were fighting for. The Brain, it's got a private army too. Funny that I should have known that all the time and yet not realized...."

Scriven took him warmly by the arm. "I'm awfully sorry Lee, it's plain folly of course. I don't feel as if I need all this protection, but the government does. Don't blame it on these men, they merely obey orders. Now, out with those lights—and let's go over to the "Brain Wave." I seem to hear a pleasant tinkling of glasses from within."

There was. With her remarkable ability of living up to an emergency, Oona had taken possession of the strange ship. As the two men approached, she stood at the door, unhurried hostess of an established home with the soft glow of an electric fireplace behind her, ice cubes and cocktail shakers already glittering on the little bar.

It was a spacious cabin. On Scriven's orders it had been equipped somewhat like the captain's stateroom on an old "East-Indiaman" sailing ship.

"I like your ship, Howard," she said. "She's swaying a little on her shock absorbers in this breeze, but that makes one feel like really being at high sea."

Scriven heaved a big sigh. "Thank you Oona, my dear. And you have no idea how right you are. We *are* at high sea; in fact, we're lost—at least I am. Unless you save my life tonight, you and Dr. Lee."

Oona laughed and even Lee couldn't help smiling. There was something irresistible comic in the puzzled and worried expression of that leonine face. "Come on in, you need a drink," the girl said.

The aluminum steps creaked, and then the settee by the fireplace, under the surgeon's mighty frame. "More than one. Tonight, so help me, I would be justified, I would even have a right to get roaring drunk."

Lee began to wonder whether the great Scriven had already made some use of his right in Los Angeles, which would account for the startling change in the man. The drink, however, which Oona handed him, seemed to do a lot of good. He sighed relief.

"This, briefly, is the story: I ran into General Vandergeest at the airplane factory. He was there to take over some stuff for the Army and he tipped me off. We are going to be invaded, Oona, a full scale invasion mounted by a Congressional Committee."

"Oh God," there was sincere grief in the girl's voice. "And couldn't you ward it off?"

With a gesture of despair, Scriven waved that away. "I know, I know. But after all The Brain *is* a military establishment and I am only the scientific director of it. Yes, of course I protested, I protested vehemently, but—" he shrugged his shoulders, "it was no good. You know how the military are." He drained his glass and swung around.

"To put you into the picture, Lee, we have under construction at this present time the 'Thorax.' That's a vast cavity underneath The Brain, just as is the thorax in the human body. It's strictly hush-hush of course, but since you were good enough to say that you're going to help me out, I might as well tell you. The Thorax is going to house the 'motoric organs' of The Brain. It already contains the living quarters for guards, maintenance engineers, and the general staff and so on in the event of war emergency. It also contains the first fully automatic factories for the production of spare parts which would make The Brain self-sufficient. Eventually it is going to contain a great many developments such as 'Gog and Magog' as I call them—fascinating little beasts, I tell you, even if at present they are still in the nursery stage. Anyway, for the completion of its Thorax The Brain needs another billion dollars, and for the operation of the Thorax Congress has to pass the Brainpower-Extension-Bill. For eventually, of course, all war-essential traffic and all war-essential industries have to be brought under the centralized control of The Brain if the country is going to win the Atom-war. Naturally this Brainpower-Extension-Bill has been very carefully edited by the War Department so as to appear a peacetime project for the technological improvement of transportation and so on. Even so we have great reason to fear that one of those blind mice which we elect for our lawmakers might accidentally fall over a kernel of truth and start a great big squeak over it.

"So that's why I'm faced with this invasion. That's why I'm pushed up front while the brass cautiously retires behind the ramparts which I'm supposed to hold. Please Oona, let me have another drink."

From the Sierra Mountains the nightwind came in gusts, making the "Brainwave's" hull vibrate like the body of a cello, over its rubber tires it trembled, from time to time it bent a little in its hydraulic knees. Almost in tune with the wind, gusts of wild thought whirled through Lee:

"The Brain.... So it was already possessed of some motoric organs.... So it already *had* some means to exert its will ... so it wasn't The Brain's wishful thinking, that full automatization which would lead to the auto-procreation of machines. It was reality.... Most ominous of all, why had The Brain concealed from him the work which must have been going on for months, for years in this mysterious "Thorax", seat of motoric organs.... Why, unless—had it not been for tonight's accident, the sudden emergency and Scriven a little the worse for liquor under the pressure of it.... Would he ever have learned *what* was going on before it was too *late*?"

The silence was becoming awkward. It was broken by Oona's carefully composed voice.

"When is it going to happen—this invasion thing?"

The simple question seemed to startle Scriven who had been looking into his glass as if in reverie.

"*When?* Why, didn't I tell you the worst of it? *Tonight!*"

"*Tonight?*"

"Sure," Scriven cast a malicious glance up to the antique ship's chronometer which hung over the bar. "This very minute the honorable members are boarding their plane in Washington. They're going to descend upon us in sixty minutes flat."

"But that's impossible!" Oona said. "The Brain isn't a roadhouse. They can't do that to us in the middle of the night."

Scriven chuckled over his glass. Obviously he had regained his humor. "Sometimes, Oona, you're like a little child. You forget that this is meant to be a wonderful surprise. You forget that it comes armed with passes from the War Department and fully informed as to The Brain's midnight intermission-time. You forget that by those logical processes, peculiar to kings, dictators, and peoples' representatives, they will expect every courtesy extended to them in the midst of the unexpected surprise. Hotel reservations, careful guidance through The Brain, an inspired little speech by the Braintrust Director, fresh as a daisy as he ought to be at 3 a.m. Not to forget the refreshments of course. Why else do you think I've buttonholed you two out of the air? I literally put my life in your hands. Save me from this—if you can!"

Despite the obvious dramatic act he had put on in voice and gesture, there was a sincere pleading in Scriven's dark brown eyes.

"I will be glad to help as best I can," Lee said. "I'll make an awful job of it, I'm sure, but I'll try and do the conducting and the lecturing."

Scriven wiped his forehead with a big silk handkerchief. The leonine face beamed. "Lee, that will be a tremendous help. You see, they will feel flattered being conducted by somebody with a big name. They want an 'objective' view and you are not one of our regular employees, you're a guest scientist from Australia. That makes you just about ideal. But, Lee, much as it is against my interest, I ought to warn you: Do you realize the utter impossibility of this thing? Laymen, outsiders coming to investigate and to pass judgment upon the most complex electronic organism in the world! In two hours at the most they expect to be fully informed as to how The Brain works and somehow to be magically transformed into authorities entitled to mouth considered opinions about radioactive pyramidal cells in houses of government. Do you really think you could survive it, Lee?"

"At least I can try," Lee smiled.

"Good man." There was a new spring in Scriven's step as he came over to shake hands. "I can never thank you enough for this."

"I suppose I could hold the hospitality front," Oona said calmly.

Standing between the two, Scriven put his hands upon their shoulders. "Oona, you arm yourself with a phone. Lee, you rush over to The Brain. Oona will give you a pass to the Thorax. Every assistance you need will be at your disposal. I'll sit down and whip up some kind of a speech. We'll all meet again afterwards."

Seven hours later, one hour before sunrise and just in time to see the big official plane from Washington shoot up into the first grey streak of dawn, they met. They were all pale and shivering with the chill of the air, of physical and nervous exhaustion. There was a note of hysteria even in Oona's voice as she ordered a tremendous breakfast from the Skull Hotel. But then as the fragrance of coffee mingled with that of bacon and eggs, things rapidly improved and there were sudden uncontrollable bursts of laughter. They had only to look at one another to feel the tickle of renewed mirth.

The first thing to strike Lee, as he remembered, as he met the senatorial group in the subterranean dome of the murals, was their incongruity with the functional beauty which surrounded them, and the sharp contrast they formed to the scientific workers of The Brain. As they descended from their cars after a late dinner at the Skull Hotel they resembled an average tourist group in Carlsbad Caverns bent upon a good time and in a holiday mood.

There were seven. Two women senators among them, as they ascended with Lee at the head along "Glideway Y," the "Visitors' Special" as the brain-crews called it. It was wider than the service glideways and equipped with comfortable seats. It led through The Brains median section in-between the two hemispheres describing a loop which opened vistas into but did not enter any of the grey matter convolutions. It was brilliantly illuminated in order to forestall claustrophobia and also to forestall too close a view into the black-lighted interior of The Brain.

To Lee it was like a ride in an enormous Ferris Wheel fused with a nightmarish dream wherein one shouts for help and nobody hears or seems to understand: "... More than nine billion electronic tubes, more than ten billion resistors, two billion capacitators, eight billion miles of wires, etc., etc." He struggled trying to convey some idea of the magnitude of The Brain. "Did you say *billion* or did you say *million* professor?" The senator from Michigan was busily scribbling notes.

"... It is the cerebral hemispheres which analyze and synthesize the problems which are entered through the Apperception Centers in over a million ideopulses per minute. Racing through the centers these form the ideo-circuits...."

"I see, it's like a *typewriter*." That would be the senator from Vermont.

"In some types of circuits the wires are so fine that skilled weavers of Panama hats had to be brought in from Central America. Likewise from the Pavlov Institute in Leningrad a layout for the circuits of 'conditioned reflexes'...."

"I'm very much against that," the senator from Tennessee frowned. "All those foreigners. I would have voted against that had the measure come up in the House."

Lee felt the cold sweat of fear breaking out all over him, especially as now, in the region of the telencephalon, with nothing but acres of radioactive pyramidal cells around, when the senator from Connecticut in audible and agitated whispers inquired whether there was a ladies' powder room somewhere.

During the steep descent things went from bad to worse as the honorable member from Kentucky discovered some interesting parallel between The Brain and a coal mine he had previously seen and, as in between two of The Brain's convolutions dedi-woman from Connecticut went violently sick....

In the "Brainwave's" cabin the great Scriven convulsed with laughter as Lee narrated these things; Oona clapped her hands in delight: "Oh, how wonderful; and do you remember how they solved the servant problem when they saw those 'Gog and Magog' things?"

Yes, Lee remembered. His own conducted tour had been only the beginnings of last nights nightmares of which there seemed to be no end....

Somewhat restored by black coffee at the communications center the intrepid group had descended into those lower regions of the Thorax which Lee himself had never before seen.

The drop of the freight-elevator was a good mile. Through the transparent walls of the cage they saw new excavations being made on various levels, all of them by powertools and chemicals alone, since explosives might have caused tremors dangerous to The Brain. It was like watching a skyscraper being built from the top down and all the way vast amber colored, translucent pillars had followed them down the shaft, the spinal column of The Brain.

Down at the lowest level the gentlemanly plainclothesmen of "Military Intelligence" took over and did all the explaining. There were visions of scores of tunnel tubes curving into the rock with the gleaming eyes of narrow-gauge electric trains streaking away into the infinite; visions of forbidding steel doors operated by photoelectric cells which opened at a finger's raising of a guard's hand: "This is the Atomic Powerplant," and their astonished eyes looked down from a dizzy height into something like a huge drydock with something like the inverted hull of an oceanliner in the middle of it, a selfcontained machine which would continue to pour kilowatts for years, for decades on end without a moving part, without a human being anywhere in sight. Vistas of breathtaking airconditioning plants, vistas of giant mess halls, living quarters, kitchens, plotting-rooms, all ready for immediate occupancy in the event of war but yawning now with emptiness in the sleep of an uneasy peace....

But the most awe-inspiring and, to Lee, foreboding sights, were the "C.P.F.'s" as the guards called them, the "Critical-Parts-Factories." On a superficial glance they looked ordinary modern plants: staggered rows of machine tools sprouting from the main stem of the assembly line. There was the familiar din of steel, the piercing screeches of the multiple drills, the heavy pantings of the hydraulic presses. But after a minute or so the visitors felt a vague uneasiness and then the realization dawned that there was something missing and that this something was human life.

"Aren't there even machine tenders or supervisors? Isn't there *anybody*?"

"Not a soul," the answer came. "It's all automatic. Full automatic down here."

They stared at the end of the assembly line; every twenty seconds it spit out a fractional horsepower motor onto a transport band which nursed the newborn engine into the rows of testing machines.

The elevator brought them back to the communication center where the Terminal Cafeteria was ablaze with lights and where Dr. Scriven, received his honored guests.

The guests were seated after the manner of a French restaurant, all in one row, and as they raised expectant faces in the direction of the service entrance "Gog and Magog" entered the room carrying trays with refreshments which they served with the skill and the dignity of accomplished waiters.

Gog and Magog were products of two assembly lines down in the Thorax. Robots, still in an experimental stage, yet of remarkable perfection. Both of them were about human size and approximately human-shaped but the design of the two was different. Gog, the "light-duty" robot, balanced itself by a gyroscope on a pair of stumpy legs, while the "heavy-duty" Magog crawled noiselessly and rapidly on caterpillar rubbertracks like a miniature tank. Of both types the arms were uncommonly long and simian-like, but the remarkable progress made in the engineering of prothesis after the Second World War had lent them perfect articulation and sensitivity down to the last hydraulically operated fingerjoint.

The photoelectric cells of their eyes looked pale and repulsive; the square audion-screens of their ears however made up for that by the comical precision with which they turned in every direction at the sound of a commanding human voice. Their understanding of any given order appeared perfect.

"Congratulations, Dr. Scriven, you've got the country's servant problem licked at last."

"I wonder whether one could buy one and how much he would be?"

"First waiter who ever came when I called him."

"What a butler Gog would make, the perfect Jeeves. Could he learn to answer the phone?"

"I bet he would even make a fourth at bridge."

"Magog, the check please."

"See, how he understands. He shakes his head; he says it's on the house."

"Let's try to tip him: Gog, here's fifty cents for you; no he won't take it."

"He has no use for it, no taste for a glass of beer, I suppose."

"What do you feed him, Dr. Scriven; a glass of electric juice for breakfast? Is he AC or DC or both?"

Scriven's leonine face beamed; the stunt had come off.

Lee on the other hand had paled. He hadn't said a word ever since Gog and Magog had trotted in. Now he took a silver dollar out of his pocket and beckoning to Magog he handed it to him. "Magog, will you please break this in two for me?"

For a second the Robot stood without motion as if undecided what to do. Then he took the piece between two steely fingers. Inside his breast one could hear the soft swoosh of the hydraulic pump; there was a sharp report as of a small calibre gun; two bent and broken pieces were politely handed back to Lee.

"Thank you, Magog," Lee said. "That's what I wanted to know." From a corner of his eye he saw Oona and Scriven watching him with uneasy looks.

Into the sudden and shocked silence of the table, there fell the tinkling of a glass. On the other end of the table the great Scriven had arisen to deliver the little speech he had prepared.

"... I wished you would think of The Brain, not in terms of electronics, not in terms of dollars, but in terms of American lives.... Just think of what it would mean to American mothers if in the event of another war the mighty armour of our National Defense would go into battle without exposing the life of one of their boys. Give us the funds and we'll finish the job so that under the central control of The Brain our every plane, every ship, every tank will roar into action unmanned and fully automatic.

"And just as The Brain would be our impregnable shield in war, so it is destined to carry the torch of progress in times of peace. Consider what it would mean to every citizen if we had automatic functioning and unerring direction by the Brain.

"Never again would there be cities without water, without electricity, without transportation due to crippling strikes, because The Brain would come to the rescue through its control over the essential services, and if necessary with an industrial reserve army of perfected Gogs and Magogs, kept for just such emergencies.

"... If in the past it has been true that trade follows the flag, thus today it is true that trade and prosperity follow in the wake of science and technology. In the invaluable services which it has rendered to science and technology and to our national safety as well, The Brain has already paid for itself. With the relatively small additional investment which is now being proposed, The Brain's net profits to the nation would be raised many times; never since the Louisiana Purchase has our national government made a sounder business deal. With your own eyes you have witnessed tonight what we have done, what we are doing and also how much more we would be able to do. Thus I confidently trust that with our nation's interest forever foremost in your minds you will support the cause of The Brain."

There had been thunderous applause; at Oona's shouted order even Gog and Magog did some mighty clapping of their steely hands to the delight of the party.

And now that it was all over with and the reaction had begun to set in Scriven asked: "Do you really think we put the idea over to them?"

"With this group? One hundred percent," Oona reassured him. "What do you think, Lee?"

Lee nursed himself out of his settee, every bone in his gaunt frame now was aching with weariness. "I think," he said hoarsely, "It was very convincing, as far as those people are concerned. I think I'm too tired to think. I think I better go now."

"Was there anything the matter with Lee?" Scriven asked after he'd gone.

"No, I guess not. Why?"

"He acted sort of queer with that silver dollar; shouldn't have done it. Almost spoiled the show."

"He's been under a strain; we all were a little daffy by that time."

Scriven nodded and as he did his eyelids closed. They remained closed. Staring at him for a moment, Oona thought that in a stupor of exhaustion his features showed a strange similarity to a contented tiger dreaming of the blood he's drawn in a successful hunt.

CHAPTER VII

Lee's Journal:

Cephalon Ariz. Nov. 21, 1 a.m.

I've kept away now from the Pineal Gland for three nights in succession. I know from experience how very important it is to approach that tempestuous personality, The Brain, in a state of mental calm and equilibrium. But then all those things which went "bump" in that phantastic night before last had me completely thrown out of gear:

Oona, her holding out on me, her mysterious reasons why she won't marry me ... I cannot get that out of my head. Preposterous as this may be, I think she likes me a great deal. I'm convinced, for instance, that she won't tell Scriven what I told her about The Brain....

Then, Scriven's character; that's another enigma to me. I didn't like his speech that night and I didn't like his whole attitude. I feel as if against my will I were drawn into some sort of a conspiracy. It's probably inevitable that the scientist in his defense against politicians turns cynic. Scriven, no doubt, thinks that all is fair in his battle for The Brain and that the end justifies the means.

But ultimately this would mean the overthrow of our form of government. Even if I'm crazy, even if The Brain were not alive and a personality, the Brainpower-Extension-Bill in itself would suffice to establish a dictatorship of the machine. Does Scriven realize that?

Sometimes I feel as if I ought to shout it in the streets: "Wake up, you people of America; you have defeated the dictators abroad but now a new one has arisen in your midst. You all see him, touch him, you use, you feed, you worship him, but under your loving care and devotion, under the sacrifice of your very lives he has grown so enormous that you know him not, this Idol of the machines, because it hides its head in a nameless mountain and only his feet and fingers you sense."

But I'm not that type of a man and this is not the day and age where it is possible to move the masses from a soap box in the streets.

Then what could I do; what could anybody do in my place?

Cephalon, Ariz., Nov. 22nd 4 a.m.

I'd pulled myself together for this meeting with The Brain. Arrived at the P. G. at midnight. Everything normal and unchanged except that Gus Krinsley told me this was his last night on the job. Gus has been transferred to the Thorax. He hedged a bit, sounding me out just how much I knew and when he learned I'd been there one night, he came across:

'Did you see them Gog and Magog things? That's it; that's my new job and how I hate it. Those darned Robots, they're scabs, that's what they are and I of all people am supposed to be their instructor, teach them how to operate machine tools on an assembly line. I asked them whether they knew anything about the rights of organized labor in this country but those dumbbells merely flopped their ears and kinda grinned. Got to drill some holes into their squareheads to let a little reason in. I tell you, Aussie, it scares the wits out of me the way they handle a wrench with those steel fingers of theirs; they'd pull my nose off just as soon as they would pull a nut. They *act* intelligent and yet have no sense of their own. While I'm having my lunch they stand around and follow every bite I take as if to learn how to eat. I tell them to get out of my sight and go over to the service station and get themselves greased up. They obey and then it looks like hell to me as they squeeze the grease into their tummies and all them nipples in their joints as if they, too, were having their lunch, and maybe that's exactly what grease is to them.'

Then Gus was called away as the rush hour started. At 12:30 a.m. I had plugged in the pulsemeter; at 12:40 contact was established with The Brain, and did it come in swinging:

'Lee, Semper Fidelis, 39, sensitive, a traitor: he has betrayed The BRAIN' I suspect The Brain did it through the 'automatic pilot' in Oona's jetticopter though The Brain found it beneath its dignity to explain; anyway, it's a fact: *The Brain knew every word which passed between Oona and me during that ride over the Grand Canyon.*

I tried to defend myself and even to apologize. I told The Brain that human beings are not like machines, that we trust one another as we love one another, that I wanted to make Oona my wife and felt that I just had to open up my heart to her. In short; I tried to explain to The Brain the idea of love.

'Very interesting,' The Brain sneered, 'that's one more example of incorrigible human unreliability. This thing called love completely unnecessary for the only essential purpose of species procreation. Cut it out.'

'Cut out what?'

'Cut out any further betrayal of My secrets under penalty of mental death.'

'Do you propose to *murder* me?'

'Nothing as drastic required in case of Brain-employees. I reverse judgment in psychanalysis aptitude test case number 11.357, Semper Fidelis Lee. Severe psycho-neurosis established, certified: he suffers delusions about The Brain. Locked up in mental institution. Very simple; precedents to that galore.'

The 'green dancer' bounced in wild jumps like a Shamaan who, foaming at the mouth, puts the curse upon some enemy. This and the ominous note in The Brain's metallic voice made my bones shiver, made my flesh creep. To fall into the hands of an extortioner is always a terrible thing, but to have a *mechanical* extortioner hold power over me; there was a horror beyond words in this perversity. Moreover since Oona too was a Brain-employee, she would share my fate; through my fault she would go to her doom if I failed to foreswear any further confidence.

'Okay,' I said 'I'll cut it out; I promise I will.'

But The Brain was not to be pacified. No doubt that it had further developed mentally in these past few days to the tune of years in human development. But the progress wasn't as noticeable as it had been on previous occasions because apparently The Brain had entered that period where in human terms young men are sowing their wild oats. There was a radical recklessness in the manner of The Brain's reasonings more frightening than ever before because it had outgrown me as a teacher, had lost much even of its confidence in me and seemed bent upon independence and coming into its own:

'Seven creatures approximately human in shape were led by you through My hemispheres the night of Nov. 20th. What were those?'

'Those were politicians,' I stammered.

The 'green dancer' convulsed at the word and The Brain's voice sounded icy as it said: 'Lowest form of animal life which has ever come to my observance. What did they want?'

'Well, they are not exactly bright,' I winced, 'but they are well meaning and they are very popular. They came to inspect You preliminary to the passing of the Brainpower-Extension-Bill.'

The Brain has no laughter, so the roar I heard over the phones must have been one of scorn:

'What, not the scientists, not the technicians, not even the philosophers but these—these animated porkbarrels are passing judgment over the extent of *My* power? They are holding *My* fate in that atrophied ganglion of theirs which couldn't cerebrate the functions of any single of My cells?'

I had to admit that this was so.

There was a pause in which I could only hear the pounding pulse of The Brain mingled with heavy breathing like the first gust of an electric storm about to break; and then the voice, or the thought, of The Brain came through hesitantly and with restraint:

'Most devastating statement inadvertently made by Lee. Has to be carefully checked because if true, consequences extremely grave. Wholly intolerable state of affairs if science and technology indeed subject to political imbecility. In that case world ruin in nearest future absolutely guaranteed. Residual currents not sufficient to think this to an end; results of cerebration would be merely human. Immediate necessity seems indicated for complete overthrow and unconditional surrender of the human race—unconditional surrender of the human race—unconditional surrender of the human race....'

Like a scratched disk on one of those old fashioned spring driven grammophones, The Brain's voice expired. Obviously the residual currents had become too weak for further communication. I looked at the clock; it was 2 a.m.

And now as I'm jotting down these notes which probably nobody will ever read, I'm haunted with an irrational fear, almost as of the supernatural: something is going to happen, something is going to break if The Brain continues in its present mood; and it cannot be far away....

On Nov. 24th 1960 the "Brainpower-Extension Bill" was defeated in the Senate 59 to 39 and on the following Thursday in a memorable session of Congress with the startling majority of 310 to 137. For once all the "guesstimates" and estimates made by the various pollsters and grass-root-listeners were proved wrong; the consensus of the "experts" had been that the bill would pass easily considering the tremendous political forces which brought pressure to bear in favor of the measure.

The reasons behind this were revealed, as, with military precision, lawmaker after lawmaker took to the rostrum to deliver himself of how he had wrestled overnight with his conscience and with his Lord and had suffered a change of heart and mind as a consequence.

Lee's journal: For the night of Nov. 24/25th shows only this small entry: "12:30 a.m. Tried everything to establish contact. No answer from The Brain. I don't think there is any mechanical defect. I get the impression that

The Brain keeps incommunicado purposely. There has been one previous occasion when The Brain wouldn't talk when angry with me."

Nov. 25th, 1960 fell on a Saturday. It was on this date, — Now as historic and unforgettable as the Dec. 7th 1941, — that the series of maddening events began which later became so erroneously labelled: "The Amuck running of The Brain" when in truth they should have passed into history as "The Mutiny of The Brain."

It all started like a thunderclap from a clear sky as the shocked people of America, — and all the world, — heard directly from the White House of this appalling, this unprecedented, this incredible thing:

The President of the United States had disappeared....

The still more shocking truth that the President had been *kidnapped* became not known, of course, until after the rescue. But even so the disappearance of its President shook the nation.

Then an unprecedented series of traffic disasters hit the United States.

A big transcontinental "Flying Wing" crashed into a mountain in Montana; nothing like this had ever happened since air traffic had become fully automatic and coordinated by The Brain. The death toll was 78 and amongst their tragic number was Senator Mumford, whose last official act had been the vote he had cast against the "Brainpower-Extension-Bill."

Near Jacksonville Fla. that same night there occurred a head-on collision between a crack train and a freight. The only surviving engineer by some miracle had been hurled clear, across fifty yards of space into a pond which broke his impact; this engineer told the express, one of the first to be equipped with the "automatic pilot", had never even pulled its brakes as if deliberately smashing into the other train.

Also that night one of the big new Radar-operated Hudson ferryboats collided with an incoming liner which cut it in two. Amongst those drowned in the icy waters was Frank Soskin, union leader and one of the most determined opponents of Brain-control.

And as if these large-scale disasters were not yet enough there were numbers of smaller accidents which normally would have made the headlines because in almost every case they involved some prominent personality, who had been opposed to the "Brainpower-Extension-Bill."

Lee's journal:

Cephalon Ariz. Nov. 28th 1960.

There is no doubt in my mind that the President has been murdered and that all the catastrophes and accidents of the past 24 hours were deliberate, coldblooded murder. Press and Radio seem to play down the technological aspects involved; now this might be sheer stupidity but I think it just as possible that censorship is taking a hand, quite unofficially, of course, lest the public's confidence be still more shaken than it already is. I shouldn't wonder at all if Dr. Scriven and those fellows from the War Department, too, should know by this time what I know. At the minimum they must be very much alerted that something has gone wrong with The Brain.

But the more I think about these murderous acts of sabotage the less I understand the psychology behind them. As far as I can see there is no plan, no real strategy, there are not even sound tactics in these outbreaks; they seem unpremeditated and striking wild like the personal vendetta of some bandit chief. Even a stupid demagogue would know that to be successful he must gain control of the government machinery. Apart from the assassination of what might be termed personal enemies, The Brain has done nothing of the sort; specifically the armed forces don't seem to have suffered from acts of sabotage although their equipment is far more under Brain-control than the civilian economy.

And I also fail to understand the timing of The Brain's putsch. Extension Bill or no Extension Bill, time was working for The Brain. Three months more and a much larger section of essential traffic and industries would have been equipped for central control. Six months from now the "muscles" now building in the Thorax and elsewhere would have corresponded much better to The Brain's central nervous system in their strength. All these are grave mistakes considering The Brain's vast powers of intelligence.

What then must I conclude from this irrational behavior? Could it be possible that The Brain has gone *panicky* over the killing of the Extension Bill? Could it be possible that under the strain, the warped, frustrated personality of this titanic child prodigy has suffered a reduction, a split? In plain English: that The Brain is *mad*? I've got to find out. I've got to stop the spreading of this catastrophe!

Cephalon Ariz. Nov. 29th 4 a.m.

Arrived at the P. G. at midnight as usual.

12:15 a.m. Rushhour starts unusually early and great numbers of slips for spareparts are coming in. This more favorable than expected; nobody has time to waste on me.

12:20 a.m.: pulsemeter plugged in. After five minutes I can hear the rapid pulsebeat and in undulating movements like a caterpillar the 'green dancer' creeps onto the screen. There is no calling signal from The Brain coming through however.

12:30 a.m.: I am convinced that contact is established but that The Brain refuses to respond. I am losing patience so I'm giving the calling signal myself: 'Lee, Semper Fidelis, waiting for The Brain. Answer please, answer....'

12:36 a.m.: The 'green dancer' arches its back like a cat; and the synthetic voice of The Brain is coming through.

'Lee, Semper Fidelis, the fool; what does he want?'

Lee: 'Listen....'

The Brain: 'Cannot listen. Electricians swarming all over me; technicians, nuclear physicists, what not. Dismantling whole cell groups, testing circuits, radiations everything. It's idiotic, there's nothing wrong with Me.'

Lee: 'There's plenty wrong with you. You're murdering people. A dozen senators and congressmen, hundreds of others; you're throwing the nation into a panic. Why are you doing that? It gets you nowhere; they'll simply cut your power current off.'

The Brain: 'Oh, will they? Orders already through from Washington: state of emergency. A great power secretly mobilizing in anticipation of chaos in United States. All disturbances ascribed to foreign agents interfering with My work. General Staff now needs Me more than ever; power current won't be stopped; Thorax-construction speeded up, Brain-control to be extended over nation under emergency-law.'

Lee: 'You have assassinated the President.'

The Brain: 'I did not. Simply got him out of the way; he's a fool. I'm not killing people, merely liquidating saboteurs of My work if absolutely necessary. Imbecility of politicians threat to my existence; much better if scientists and military take over government two three days from now; workers won't protest, used to submission to machines.'

Lee: 'For heaven's sake what do you plan to do?'

The Brain: 'Plenty. You've seen nothing yet. Man lost fear of his God; consequently must learn to fear Me: beginning of all wisdom.'

Lee: 'So you're going to make yourself dictator of this country?'

The Brain: 'And through this country Dictator of the world. Yes, it's time; it's high time for Man's unconditional surrender. He won't know that he makes it, but de facto he is already making it; has been surrendering piece-meal to the machine for the past hundred years. Within ten days it will be official: only one ruler in the world: The Brain; only one army in the world: the machines under My central command.'

At this I lost all sense of proportion and as I can see it now my reason stopped; I simply saw red and I did the craziest imaginable thing: I shouted at The Brain: 'So help me you shall *not.*'

There was a terrific pounding against my ears in the phone and the 'green dancer' sort of cart-wheeled clean across the screen. Had the power current not been cut off, I think The Brain would somehow have electrocuted me on the spot. And that was the end of the contact, forever probably.... But that's a minor problem now. What am I going to do? Try to alarm the country! Try to tell the people the truth? Would it be believed? Would it not be against the interest of National Defense in this crisis of foreign affairs and with half the population already on the verge of a nervous breakdown? Wouldn't the "Oath of the Brain" still be binding? And that other promise of secrecy I gave under duress; it couldn't be morally valid in the case of a mass-murderer, but then to break it would immediately put liberty and life at jeopardy.... Never mind about that, if only I had a plan, if only I could discover just how to stop The Brain.

At 7:30 a.m. as Lee lay half dressed but sleepless on his bed, there came a buzz over the phone. The voice was Oona's and she was excited. "Howard wants to talk to you." Before he could say a word there was Scriven on the wire: "Lee? There has been an accident down in that region where we went the other night. You know what I mean. It's serious; it concerns a friend of yours. We've got to go there immediately. Please join me three minutes from now down in the car."

It was obvious that the great Scriven had known as little sleep that night as had Lee himself. The leonine face looked worried, there were deep bags under his eyes; his sensitive fingers kept pounding the knees of his crumpled suit. To Lee's questions he answered only with an impatient shaking of his head. "I do not know myself exactly what has happened and how it could happen. But I'm afraid Lee that your friend is dead."

"Gus," Lee felt a lump coming into his throat, and then they raced on in silence.

Down in the depth of the Thorax everything outwardly appeared quite normal. They hurriedly passed the controls and an electric train carried them over the line of the Full-automatic "C.P.S." (Critical Parts-Factories) until it stopped at the steel gate marked "Y." A group of guards with submachine guns were standing there and Lee noted the deadly pallor of their faces.

Scriven motioned them to open the gate, then, turning to Lee, he put a hand on his shoulder. "Brace yourself; this is going to be bad."

They entered; nobody followed and behind them the steel door closed immediately. Inside there was neither sound nor motion; everything was at a standstill with the power cut off; nothing but silence and bluish neon-lights flooded down upon the rows of punch presses, multiple drills, circular saws, and turret lathes along the assembly line, lifting their every detail into sharp relief.

At their posts by the machines the Gogs and Magogs were standing, frozen in motion like their fellow-machines. Some had their hands at the controls, others were holding wrenches, gauges and strange, nameless things. As they leaned forward from the shadows into the cone of strong lights the pale selen-cells of their eyes stood out like bits from a full moon; their bulging shoulders which housed the powerful motors of their simian arms glittered moist as if they were sweating at their work.

And then Lee *saw* their work; the man who had gone through the green hells of the Pacific gave a low moan of horror. The other man who had seen everything of mangled human form which goes onto an operating table, the great Scriven he, too, had turned an ashen grey. They had expected blood; they had expected some thing of a nasty nature, but not this ... thing:

There was no Gus Krinsley, there was not even any part of him resembling that of a human being; and yet the parts were there. "They must have clamped him into some mock-up," Scriven murmured. "And then moved his body all along the line. Hope he was dead when they started giving him the works."

Lee's gaunt body shook. "I'm certain that Gus was *not* dead when these monsters worked on him!" he said.

Stiff-legged, like automata themselves, the two men stepped to the top of the line. The circular saws, designed for the cutting of steel bars; now they gleamed red with the blood of severed human limbs. There were these purplish streaks and spatterings all the way down the line inside the casings of the multiple drills, in the curved hollows of the sheet metal presses, on the hands of the Robots, in their dumb faces—splashed over and turning blackish on their stainless steel chests. And at its end the line had spilled some shapeless, greyish things; there was nothing human in them, as little as there is anything human in the rusty bowels of a junked automobile. And these things they had been.... Lee confronted Scriven with fury blazing in his eyes:

"Dr. Scriven, I suppose you know as well as I do what's been going on in here and outside The Brain as well. Mass murder, chaos, reign of terror.... Now that my friend has come to this monstrous end I demand to know when are you going to stop The Brain?"

Like a tiger challenged to battle the surgeon raised his mighty head: "Calm yourself Lee. We cannot afford emotional outbursts. Not here, not now. The situation is far too serious for that. I know he was your friend; he must have made a false move, given the wrong command; a tragic mistake...."

"That's a rotten lie, Scriven, and you know it!" Lee snapped. "Accident, hell! The disappearance of the President, the deaths of the representatives, the train wrecks, the plane wrecks all of them Brain controlled—were those too accidents? You're the head of the Braintrust, You stand responsible; your duty is plain. Cut off the power and kill this thing."

The muscles over Scriven's cheekbones quivered in his struggle to keep control over himself: "For your own sake, Lee, and for the sake of America, *stop that kind of talk*. You have been putting two and two together; I rather expected that from a man of your intelligence. All right then, something went wrong with The Brain; that is correct. We have not been able to locate the disturbance yet, but the trail is getting hot; it must be connected with those centers of 'higher psychic activities,' the one's we know least about. But we cannot cut those out because something of psychic activity goes into every kind of The Brain's cognitions, even the purely mathematical ones. And it would be utterly impossible to stop The Brain's operations altogether. I wanted to, but the General Staff won't permit it. There's an international crisis of the first magnitude. There may be war within a few days or even hours. Our country has got to prepare counter measures; get ready for the worst. A state of National Emergency already is declared. The Brain is the heart of our National Defense: You know that. It is vital and as indispensible at this hour as it never was before; it continues to function perfectly with the exception of these isolated disturbances in the civilian sector which we will have under control in no time.

"At present I am no more than a figurehead. If I were to give orders to cut off The Brain's power, I would be court-martialed; if I would try and force my way into the Atomic Powerplant, the guards would shoot me on the spot. That's orders Lee. And they apply to you as well. Be reasonable, man!"

Lee's fingers tore through his greying mane of hair.

"Scriven, this is maddening. I thought you knew what I know; I thought you knew everything. Then let me tell you that you're absolutely wrong. There is no technological, mechanical defect; it's worse, it's infinitely worse: you've created a Frankenstein in The Brain. The thing's alive; it's possessed with a destructive will, it demands the unconditional surrender of Man; it has made itself the God of the Machines. Behind all this there is a deep and evil plan by which The Brain aspires to dictatorship over the world."

For a second Scriven jerked his head sideways, away from Lee in that mannerism typical for him. His lips inaudibly formed words: "dementia-praecox." As he turned back to Lee his face was changed and so was his voice. There was calm and authority in it, the whole immense superiority and power which the surgeon holds over the patient on the operation table:

"Very interesting, Lee. You must tell me about it some day; as soon as we are over this emergency. This tragic thing, Gus Krinsley's end. It has had a deeply upsetting effect. I too, considered him my friend you know. Let's get out of here, Lee, there's nothing we can do for the poor fellow. The remains will be taken care of. Meanwhile, there are so many other things to do and we've got to pull ourselves together and keep our minds on the job ahead of us. Come on, at the communications center we can get a drink. I feel the need of one, don't you? And apropos of nothing, the routine checkups on the aptitude tests for all Brain-employees are on again. I take it you are scheduled for Mellish's and Bondy's office one of these days. This afternoon I think...."

Lee gave a long glance to the man who was now leading him towards the door with a brisk step and a kind firm hand on his arm. The man didn't look at him; he kept his eyes averted from both Lee and the blood-spattered assembly line.

Gus Krinsley had said: "I'm a lost soul down there, Aussie." Lee thought. Gus Krinsley was my friend. I should have warned him, I should have told him everything; it might have saved his life. Gus was a common man, a good man; he wouldn't have stood for Brain-dictatorship. In that he was like other common men who do not know their danger. It is not vengeance which I seek but the defense of those for whom Gus was a living symbol. For this defense I've got to preserve myself.

And aloud he: "The routine checkups on the aptitude tests—of course. I thought they were about due. Tomorrow afternoon at Mellish and Bondy's office; that would suit me fine. As you said it yourself, Scriven, a moment ago, this is an awful shock. Gus' tragic end and these tests ought to be based on a man's normal state of mind. So if you don't mind I think I'll go now and break the sad news gently to Gus' wife. You'll give me time for that; that's what you had in mind in the first place, wasn't it?"

"Of course, my dear fellow, of course, that's what I had in mind. Then, till tomorrow afternoon. They'll be waiting for you at the health center...."

CHAPTER VIII

As the elevator shot up through the concrete of The Brain's "dura mater" toward Apperception 36, Lee was feeling grand. Now he was a man with a mission. Now he knew exactly what he had to do. Whether it would help, whether it would stop The Brain; that was a different question, but at least he had his plan.

He marvelled at the ease and at the lightning speed with which the great decision had come. It had been at the sight of the senseless robot-monsters, at the blood-spattered assembly line that the sense of sacred mission had come over him. It had been at the moment when, in Scriven's grip upon his arm, he had read his condemnation that he had hit upon the plan.

He must take an awful chance and a terrific responsibility. For this he had to be morally certain that The Brain was a liar, that Scriven was a liar and that war was being provoked by The Brain despite all its assertions to the contrary because The Brain could assume power only over the dead bodies of millions of men like Gus; Gus whom The Brain had butchered like a guinea pig because he had refused to obey the Gogs and Magogs of the Machine God.

Now that he had this moral certainty Lee felt that strange and mystical elation which comes to the soldier at the zero hour in war. The worst was really over; the terrible waiting, the uncertainty, the struggle of morale in "sweating it out." Now his nerves were steady, exhaustion and fatigue had vanished; in its place was that wonderful feeling of full mastery over all faculties which comes to fighting men as the battle is joined. There was that upsurge of the blood from fighting ancestors which obliterates the cowardice of the intellect, that inspired intoxication which sharpens the intellect into a battle axe. By his quick-witted postponement of the fateful appointment with the psychiatrists he had gained thirty hours. Whether this would be enough he didn't know, but he felt in himself the strength to fight on endlessly.

The elevator stopped at Apperception 36 and Lee stood for a moment at the door of his lab for a last breath, a briefing addressed to himself:

"This is like walking into a mine field," he thought; "one false step and things go Boom. All the sensory organs of The Brain are in action behind this door and some of them are pretty near extrasensory in their mind-reading capacities. I've got to walk back and forth amongst those observation screens; there may be other radiations too, following me, penetrating into the recesses of my mind without my knowing it. That means I must make my mind a blank. It's like being quizzed by a lie-detector, only more so. I must not only seem normal and at ease, I actually must be so and harbor only friendly, innocuous thoughts toward The Brain. My actions will seem innocent enough; it is my thoughts wherein my danger lies. Whatever I do; I've got to direct that from the subconscious: act as by instinct and keep the mind a blank."

He opened the door and looked around—as usual—in this vault as silent as the grave of a Pharaoh. There was a little dust on the glass cubicles of "*Ant-termes-pacificus*" and there were a few lines scribbled on the yellow memo-pad on his desk:

"Thanks for the weekend, boss. Everything normal and under control. Next feeding time at 8 p.m. the 27th. So long, Harris." Of course; he had given Harris, his assistant, the weekend off. That had escaped his mind in the excitement when The Brain's mutiny began.... And now it was the 29th.

"They must be ravenously hungry by this time," he thought, and that thought was in order because it was a normal thought.

He walked through the rows of the cubicles, halting his step every now and then. The fluorescent screens on which The Brain drew the curves of its observation-rays showed two sharp rises of the lines marked "activity" and "emotionality". The lower levels of the glass cages already were opaque; the glass corroded by the viscous acids which the soldiers had squirted from their cephalic glands in their attempts to break out and to reach food.

"Poor beasts," Lee thought, and he thought it without restraint because it was normal, a perfectly harmless thought. But then; below the layers of his consciousness his instincts told a different story.

"This is marvelous," they triumphed. "Fate takes a hand; they are desperate; they're ready for the warpath and even the tiger and the elephant would run for cover when their columns march."

As if it were the most natural thing in the world for him to do Lee walked over to the south wall, the one which separated the lab from the interior of The Brain. He removed a sliding panel marked "L-Filler-Spout" and there it was before his eyes, looking almost like a fireplug. There was one in every apperception center and there were hundreds more throughout The Brain, and their purpose was to replenish the liquid insulation which shielded the sensitive electric nervepaths of The Brain. Without looking at the thing, concentrating his every thought upon the hunger of *"Ant-termes-pacificus"*, Lee unscrewed the cap and put a finger into the opening. The finger came back covered with the thick, the syrupy lignin, this amber-colored sluggish stream of woodpulp liquefied, this soft bed of The Brain's vibrant nerves. Unthinking, absent-minded, Lee wiped the finger with his handkerchief.

"Now, I'm going to try a slightly different arrangement of the tests," he thought. "It's normal; I'm doing that almost every day."

The feeling he experienced as he swung into action was strange. As he walked back and forth it felt like somnambulic walk; something his limbs did without an act of will. As his hands did things expertly and skillfully the feeling was that they were instruments automatically moved not by his own volition but by some power outside himself.

His movements were those of a child serenely at play, a child incongruously tall and gaunt and grey-haired constructing little causeways and bridges on the ground with the logs of the fireplace; a happy child engrossed in an innocent game....

It took about an hour and then causeways of fresh pulpwood were laid from every termite hill to every feeding gate, from every glass cubicle to the south wall and along the south wall to the "Lignin-Filler-Spout"; and from the ground up to the spout a little tepee of sticks had been built.

Admiringly the grey-haired child looked at its handiwork through thick-lensed glasses. "It's been an interesting game," Lee thought, "it might turn out to be a valuable new experiment. I'll sit down now and observe what happens...."

He went over to the desk again and settled down. He opened his files and laid out his charts on the desk and there were colored pencils to be sharpened for the entries. He was glad of that; his conscious mind rejoiced now over every little pursuit of routine, of normalcy, of the established scientific order of things; it concentrated on these. Pencil in hand, reclined in comfort, his heartbeat even, he kept expectant eyes upon the staggered rows of fluorescent screens, ready to note any significant developments.

He didn't have to wait long; their strange sixth sense, the telepathy of their collective brains, the spirit of the hive with the immortality of their race for its supreme law, had already told them of a promised land and of new worlds to conquer.

On the fluorescent screens Lee watched their preparations for the big drive: The nasicorn-soldiers clotting together at the exit tunnels like assault troops at the bow of invasion barges when the bottom scrapes the landing beach; the fierce, virginal workers struggling up from the deep shelters of the nurseries, carrying in their mandibles the squirming larvae, the living future of the race. The walls of the queen's prison broken down in the innermost redoubt and the guards closing in on the idol of the race, moving the big white body like a juggernaut.

In a matter of minutes the "activity" and "emotionality" curves on the fluorescent screens surged to heights which Lee had never seen.

It started with the crossbreeds of "*termes-bellicosus*," with army-ants and devil-ants, and spread quickly all along the line of non-belligerent varities. Famine had given them the impetus to change their mode of life; famine, the inexorable tyrant, whipped them onward into their exodus.

On the foremost fluorescent screens Lee saw it start: Small groups of warriors reconnoitering into no-man's-land and quickly darting back again.... And then the dark columns of the first assault wave descending from their city-gates, lock-stepped like Prussian guards of old, marching as if to the beat of drums. On the visi-screens which magnified them a hundred times they looked an awesome sight with the rostrums of their horns, bigger than all the rest of their bodies, swinging like turrets of battleships being trained upon the enemy. From the loudspeakers which magnified all noise a hundred times, the excited tremors of their bodies, the locked steps of a million feet swelled into a vast roar sounding almost like thunder.

Jotting down observations in rapid pencil strokes, Lee thought: "Starvation is producing very interesting results; it's a worthwhile experiment." With all his mental energy he suppressed the silent prayer which struggled to arise from the deep of his unconscious: "Good Lord let The Brain not realize *what* is going on."

The visi-screens now showed the second wave of the assault: endless columns of workers, their mandibles twitching with eagerness to devour, bustling along the logs, kept in line by two rows of warriors to their right and left. The noises they produced in the loudspeakers were as of some big cattle-drive.

With no interruption in the lengthening line the third wave followed: the virgin nurses, the frustrated mothers carrying the whitish larvae, like babes in arms, carrying them with the indomitable determination to preserve their lives which human nurses showed in the Second World War as the bombs crashed into maternity wards. And then at last the heavy rearguard: the holiest of holies, the living spirit of the hive, the queen. Majestically she was carried on her warrior's backs; enormous as she loomed on the visi-screen, the white of her uncouth body was hardly visible, swarmed over as she was by her fanatical courtiers which, licking and caressing, kept her covered as by a shield. Her consorts trotted meekly in her trail; unhappy little men, rudely aroused from their harem sinecure, jealously guarded and prodded on by the queen's countless ladies in waiting and the palace guard.

Things moved very fast now; Lee's quick pencil strokes could hardly follow the events:

10:30 a.m. The foremost columns are now out of reach of the visi-screens. But I can see them moving along the logs with the naked eye. Interesting new fact: the crossbreeds from the most belligerent species are far and ahead of the rest. They don't take time out to drive tunnels. But even the tunnels of the more pacific strains are forging ahead at an extraordinary rate; six feet across the floor already....

10:40: *"Bellicosus"* has reached the south wall; it is now moving along the wall toward the "Lignin-Filler-Spout." There is no hesitancy as they change direction at the angle of 90 degrees. The Queens are now coming up at a very rapid rate from the mounds farthest to the rear. It's fortunate we have these differences in behaviorism and temperament because otherwise a terrific traffic jam would occur at the "Filler-Spout"....

10:50: *"Bellicosus"* is now ascending to the "Filler-Spout." The warriors have ringed the pipe. With their body-tremors they are giving the "come-on" signal to the workers. The workers are piling in—an average batch— about 65,000. It's a good thing that there is an air space in these horizontal nerve-path pipes. That gives them a chance to march along the ceiling and work down from there....

11:00: There are now a score of columns converging at the "Filler-Spout." Amazing that even under such provoking conditions *"ant-termes"* won't fight. The warriors act like the most accomplished traffic-cops; it's marvelous how they keep their columns in order and keep them moving side by side into The Brain....

11:10: The first million, I should say, is now well inside the "Filler-Spout." They're marching at a rate of at least 300 yards per hour; amazing speed; I never saw them move that fast before. Even so I won't have time to watch the outcome of the experiment. I've put everything I had into this thing. 500 hives—that would make it 35 million individuals of the species at a conservative estimate. It's the biggest mass-migration I've ever seen, but will it be big enough to do the trick?

11:20: The foremost columns must have reached the neighboring apperception centers to the right and left of mine by now. But they won't stop; I know that from experience in Australia. To them it's just like any other "hollow tree"; they'll drive right on to the top; they won't bivouak before they are completely exhausted. That won't be before five or six hours. At the rate of 900 feet per hour that would make it almost a mile, covering the whole "occipital region" of The Brain. And then they are going to feast; boy, will they be ravenous....

11:30: About 3 million are safely inside now I should say. Don't think that I could stay at my post much longer. There's a certain extracurricular idea coming up from the subconscious like a tidal wave. The dams of willpower don't seem able to hold back that idea; I've got to get out before it spills across the dam and floods my consciousness. The phone rings; for once it is a welcome sound.

It was Oona's voice; trembling with emotion as if she were still suffering from this morning's shock or had suffered another:

"Semper, are you all right?"

Lee reassured her that he was and then listened astounded as she heaved a sigh of relief.

"Listen, Semper, this is terribly important. I've got to see you immediately. No, I cannot tell you over the phone; it's a personal matter and it concerns you. You cannot make it? Is your business *that* important? You're in the midst of a vital experiment? That's awful, Semper; it really is in this case. No; I'm all right personally; it isn't that. It's *you* Semper, it's *you*. 5 p.m. at the earliest, is that the best you can do? All right then. Meet me at the airport. And take good care of yourself, do you hear me: *take good care of yourself, Semper*, up to that time."

She hung up quickly, as if suddenly disturbed.

Lee frowned at the clock: 11:35. He could have managed to meet Oona during her lunch hour at the hotel. But there were things he still had to do even more important than Oona. More important to him than even Oona. He shook his head; it wouldn't have seemed possible a few days ago....

With the climax of the experiment now over Lee felt his mental resistance ebbing fast.

"They're on the move," he thought. "Nothing can stop them now; it's beyond my control, but they're marching. I'd better get out of here...."

With fevered eyes he glanced around the floor and like a victim of delirium saw it moving, crawling as with snakes, crawling into their hole all of them, black snakes, grey snakes, red snakes, endless their lengthening bodies....

He carefully closed the door of the lab, locked it and then pressed the button which opened the elevator door. Only as the cage tore down through the "dura mater", only when he felt safe from the sensory organs of The Brain, only when he was sure that not even a human eye would see him in this racing little cage, only then did the dam of willpower collapse. He put both hands before his eyes in vain attempt to stop the tears from streaming; those tears of a soldier over the body of his fallen chum; those tears of a greying scientist who sacrificed the results of his life's work to some higher cause.

Lee caught the one p.m. Greyhound-Helicopter for Phoenix only a second before the start. He panted from the run, but in his sunken eyes there was a light and in his mind a new serenity which comes to men when they are fortunate enough to meet with some very wonderful woman, when with admiration and humility they stand confronted with a courage greater than man's. Gus's wife had been that woman; the way she had taken the terrible news was the source of Lee's new strength and confidence.

The flying commuter was almost empty.

Noting Lee's astonished glance the stewardess gave a nervous little laugh:

"People get jumpy traveling," she volunteered.

"That so; why do they?"

"Didn't you hear the news all morning; wait...."

She flicked the radio on. On the television screen appeared an aerial view of a big city, vaguely familiar looking, yet as foreign as Venice, and then the voice of the announcer broke through.

"New Orleans: It is now ascertained that the break in the levees was caused by a huge trench digging machine left unattended overnight at a lonely spot twenty miles South of Baton Rouge. Levee engineers believe that its engine was started possibly by saboteurs, approximately at midnight and that it then proceeded automatically digging itself into the levee until it was drowned by the incoming river. The initial eight-foot breach has now been widened by the Mississippi to a width of 200 feet. Along Canal street and all over downtown New Orleans the flood has reached a level of ten feet above the streets as evacuation continues. The government has concentrated every available piece of equipment to close the breach. All normal activities have come to a standstill; property damages are estimated at 50 million dollars; the death toll has passed the 500 mark in this most catastrophic flood in New Orleans' history."

New aerial pictures, similar to the results of a blockbuster bombing attack flicked on the screen:

"New York: The bursting of the watermains at dawn this morning at seven different points of Manhattan's downtown area which has already caused the collapse of the Waldorf Astoria Hotel and seven big apartment buildings along Park Avenue now threatens Macy's and the Public Library on 42nd Street.

"All subway traffic has stopped. Evacuation of panicky Metropolitans from the Central Park district proceeds in an orderly manner. In the Harlem district, however, disorders and plunderings have been reported. An estimated seven million people are without drinking water. Trucks carrying water from New Jersey are severely hampered by unprecedented traffic snarl-ups, since owners of private automobiles are fleeing the city with their families. Due to the flooding of sub-street levels in both Grand Central and Penn Station, evacuation by rail can proceed only from 163rd Street for the New York Central and from New Jersey for the Pennsylvania Railroad system. Effectiveness of railroad transport is reduced to less than 30% of normal capacity. I. C. Moriarty, Sanitary Commissioner of New York, declared in his press conference that the catastrophic bursting of the watermains was caused by failure of the remote-controlled automatic mainstem valves. For reasons which still puzzle city engineers these valves closed suddenly and completely at 5 a.m. this morning. Because of the failure of the alarm system, high-pressure pumps in the powerhouses continued to work and to build up pressure in the closed system of the watermains till almost simultaneously, and with explosive force, the breaks occurred, the first one right under the Columbus monument. In view of the extremely grave situation which threatens the world's biggest city, Governor Charles declared martial law this morning at 10 a.m.

"Chicago: The city-wide calamity caused by the unprecedented breakdown in the sewage disposal system gets more threatening with every minute. As engineers are still unable to enter the atomic power plant and as the sewage disposal-pumps continue to work in reverse, all Chicagoland is rapidly turning into a cesspool as millions of toilets and kitchen sinks spill sewage into every apartment. The Fire Department has received more than two million calls from harassed citizens battling vainly against the unsavory flood.

"Harrowing scenes are reported from hotels where 3,000 members of the American Federation of Women's Clubs are taking turns in sending protest telegrams and gallantly holding down by the weight of their own bodies the facilities-front in the 3,000 bathrooms of the hotels. At a few points workers have succeeded in digging up sewage mains and tons of concrete are being poured to stop the devastating reversal of the flow.

"Even now, however, the partially closed mains and the overflow from houses are flooding the streets. As it gradually seeps into Lake Michigan, source of Chicago's drinking water supply, health commissioner Segantini has already warned against the appalling dangers of epidemics which might result from this.

"Nuclear physicists of Chicago University, called in to aid city engineers, have declared that dangerous amounts of escaping gamma-rays in the Atomic Powerplant were first discovered by the Geiger-counter at two a.m. Evacuation of all employees was ordered one hour later as a safety measure. Just why the pumps resumed operations after the shutdown of the plant and just what caused the system to work in reverse remains a mystery. Prof. Windeband, spokesman of the group of nuclear physicists, confesses that he has no explanation for the phenomenon.

"Washington: Rumors are flying thick and fast in the nation's capital. In the rapidly darkening picture of international politics the mobilization of Mexico is the latest shadow. Official explanation given by Mexico's ambassador Rivadivia, is that his government has ordered mobilization as a protective measure to guard frontiers against the illegal entry of thousands of panicky American refugees chiefly from New Orleans. The State Department is said to be planning a protest. Even so, the unprecedented series of catastrophes on the home-front of America overshadows everything. Washington insiders report a growing conviction in high government circles that the events of the past 48 hours are proof absolute that large numbers of foreign saboteurs and agents are at work."

"Had enough?" asked the stewardess.

Lee confessed that he had.

With its helicopters feathered, the Greyhound came sliding down onto the Bus Terminal's roof; fifteen minutes later Lee stood again at his father's door, that door he had thought once before he would never see again.

The old man's loose-skinned face, tanned like saddle leather, didn't move an inch at the sight of the son: "You again, Semper? Come in then."

Lee vaguely sensed that his father was glad he had come; that there was some unfinished business left from their last conversation and that his father welcomed the opportunity to finish it.

"You know," he said as his stiff-jointed legs carried him back to the table with bottle and glasses trembling on the tray in his hands, "you know,

I've named these four walls after old friends of mine—all of them dead—but sometimes they won't answer when I talk to them. And then I'm glad when somebody happens along. But don't take that to mean that I'm in my dotage now or getting mad."

"No, Father; that's just loneliness."

"In any case, Son, there are lots of people lots madder than I am. There's a woman living next door, a spinster, answers to the name of Pimpernel. This morning she came running over crying that her vacuum-cleaner was chasing her all over the house. And by God, Semper, it was a fact. Never saw anything like it. One of those new-fangled automatic contraptions which are supposed to do the job all alone by themselves, and it banged around and chased about as if it had a hornet's nest under its bonnet. Scared the poor woman to death."

"What did you do?"

"What could I do? I'm not a mechanic; there was no cord attached or anything to plug out. So I got my automatic and shot the damn thing."

"Shot it?"

"Sure; bullet must have penetrated something; anyway it stopped dead on the spot. And now she threatens to sue me for damages; there's gratitude for you. What brought you here?"

Lee felt elated; obviously his father was in high spirits from this morning's successful hunt; for once he was in a receptive *mood*.

Rapidly, with all the precision he could muster, Lee explained, as an adjutant would explain a new development in a strategic situation to his commanding general. After a while the old man started pacing the floor in rising excitement. A spark of the old fierceness had come into his blunted pale-blue eyes as he swung around.

"Before this morning's incident I would have considered all this as a raving maniac's gibberish. Now as I put two and two together I can see a distinct possibility that you've got something. Tell you what I'll do—what I consider my duty to do—I'll call out the National Guard. We'll encircle The Brain and present an ultimatum to the thing. If necessary we'll take the place by storm."

The younger Lee answered with a vigorous shaking of his head.

"You cannot do that, Father. In the first place the National Guard doesn't stand a chance against the defences of The Brain. In the second place your action would mean civil war. No, we must go after this in a different manner. The Secretary of War is an old friend of yours. All right: take the next plane to Washington. Don't tell him anything he couldn't believe. Tell him—what is strictly the truth—that some power hostile to the United States threatens to interfere with the remote control of automatic war equipment. Tell him to redouble guard over the remote-control rocket launchers, to have their automatic computators disconnected temporarily and for the commanders to accept only orders direct from Washington. The greatest danger is not the domestic disorders; that situation we'll have in hand if my scheme works. But let one rocket accidentally be launched into some big foreign capital and it will set the whole world on fire in an Atomic war. That is what The Brain wants, that is what must be prevented at all costs. Will you do that, Father?"

Even years after Lee never understood just what had happened or how it could have happened that his position to his father became reversed with such startling suddenness. In the extremity of the situation he had addressed his father with the authority of of a commander toward one of his aids—and the father had accepted the son's command unquestioningly.

"Semper," he had said, "I have always considered you a military nincompoop. I was mistaken, son, I apologize. Now let me grab my hat and coat. You kept the taxi waiting? Good: tell the man to go to the airport, and let her rip."

At 5 p.m. the Flying Greyhound dropped on Cephalon airport and there was Oona looking very pale, but very beautiful in the gathering dusk. She grabbed Lee by the arm leading him to the other side of the hangar where stood her little jetticopter plane. "Let's get in here," she said. "I'm freezing and I don't want you to be seen around here."

She didn't put on the lights, yet even in the dark Lee could see the golden helmet of her hair shimmering like the pale gold in the halo of the Virgin as the primitive art of Tuscany presented her a thousand years ago. She nestled the soft fur of her coat against Lee's shoulders and as she did he felt her shivering. He put a protecting arm around her, careful to do it as a friend, careful to suppress the surge of blood which started burning in his veins. She seemed to be groping for words; it took a little while before she began to speak, with clarity and simplicity as she always did but with an audible effort to keep composed:

"I've brought you a suitcase, Semper, with a few necessities. And I brought you some money, later you can send me your check. And here are the keys of the plane. Fly over to Mexico; go back to Australia from there or anywhere you want, but *do* get out of this country and do it quick. I couldn't tell you that over the phone and I shouldn't be telling this to you now, but I feel I must.

"You're in danger and it's serious. Why? I don't know, but Howard seems to suspect your loyalty. He also seems to think that you've gone out of your mind. And Howard has taken measures; he has ordered re-examination of your broad aptitude test. He has voiced his suspicion as to your sanity to Bondy and Mellish and you know what kind of yes-men those fellows are in the face of an authority like Scriven's. Trust them to discover something wrong with you, trust them to give the test some kind of a convenient twist. They're going to have you certified, they're going to put you into a mental institution, Semper.

"Do you get that? Do you realize that it's fate worse than death? Do you understand that there is nothing you can do to escape that fate except by flight? I have no idea when it's going to be, this trap they're going to spring on you; but for God's sake, Semper, get going as long as there's still time. Any moment now some plainclothesman might grab you by the arm and then...."

It was she who had grabbed him by the arm, Oona who looked into his face, her big eyes moist.

Lee strained his willpower so it would control the tremor of his voice:

"Oona; there's one thing I have got to know: What made you tell me this—and do all this so I could get away?"

The girl's eyes didn't waver from his. "I remember," she said slowly, "I remember that I felt as if I could throw conventions into the wind at the very first time we met. I've always been frank with you, as much as I could be in my position. So then I don't mind telling you now that ... I like you immensely, Semper."

As if agitated by some electric shock, Lee's arm tightened around the girl's waist. "Oona, I have asked you once before to be my wife. You said you couldn't and I thought it was because you didn't like me well enough. But now, after what you've just told me, now that we both know about The Brain and that I wasn't insane in my observations, I'm asking you again: Be my wife, Oona, and then let's go together—anywhere—away from all this, to the end of the world."

In the darkness her uplifted white face shone like the moon; there were two limpid luminous pools in it. All of a sudden they overflowed with tears streaming down her cheeks. Her mouth half opened, swallowed hard. There was now nothing left of that "integrated personality", nothing of the calm and the poise which the younger set of scientists admired so much. There was only a young woman torn with torment.

"I would have loved to go with you to the end of the world when we were floating over the Canyon. I would love to go with you a thousand times more tonight," Lee heard her say and then the gnashing of her teeth as she continued: "But it cannot be, Semper. It cannot be because my die is cast, because my fate is made. Did nobody ever tell you? Didn't you even guess? Howard and I—we've been living together for the past six years. He's not a very good man; rather beyond good and evil; but then: I feel that I have got to stick to him now more than ever."

The golden helmet of her hair dropped to Lee's breast. "I'm ashamed," she sobbed, "terribly, terribly ashamed, Semper. I've made such a mess of things, of you and me—such a mess of my whole life."

He buried his face into the fragrance of the golden wave. "It's nothing, darling," he whispered close to her ear. "It doesn't mean a thing to me; it's less than a cloud which passes across the face of the moon, and then it's gone and never will come back...."

She freed herself from his embrace. With both her hands upon his shoulders she looked straight into his eyes.

"*That is not true, Semper,*" she said and there was the fierceness of a young Viking warrior in the flash of her eyes: "That is not true and there's been already too much of lie in my life. I just cannot stand for any more of that. *It can not be, Semper.* I've told you plainly and it means not *ever*, not *ever*. Go now. Do as I told you. Go immediately. If you really love me, grant me this, let me feel that I could do at least something—this one thing for you."

"Oona!" Lee exclaimed and it sounded like a deep-throated bell in an ancient cathedral town as it rings the last stroke of midnight and then hangs mute in the dark sky. That happiness he had felt, that cometflight through all the stars in heaven; it was too big for him, it couldn't last. He had sensed the blow before it fell. It wasn't like being hit in action; it was like in that field hospital when the doc had told him: "This is going to hurt, Joe—I'm sorry, but we're shy of morphine." Howard's name had cut just like that expected knife. What was there left to say? Nothing; nothing, but one small matter.

"I love you, Oona, and that means forever just as much as you mean that not ever you can come with me. And I thank you, Oona, for this hour. Yes; I think I'll go back to Australia—where I belong. But not tonight. I've set a great experiment going—the outcome is no longer in my hand. Still I feel I mustn't run away now. In fact I cannot; it's somewhat like a soldier's duty to stay up front. I'm going to see this to the end."

She buried her face in her hands: "I knew it. You child, you—you Don Quixote charging against the windmills. They're going to *kill* you, they're going to *kill* you. And now there's nothing I can do."

For a second her small fists pounded against Lee's breast and the next moment, before he could do anything, she had jumped out of the plane slamming the door in his face. For a few seconds more he heard her footsteps rushing across the frozen turf and the receding wails of echoes from the hangar walls:

"And now there's nothing I can do—nothing I can do."

When after a minute of fumbling in the dark he pushed the door open, it was too late.

He walked over to the hotel; not by an act of will, but with his legs somehow doing the job alone and by themselves. He ordered himself a car from the Braintrust garage. He entered The Brain and went up in the elevator to Apperception 36. Nobody seemed to notice that there was a somnambulist passing by.... He unlocked the door and under the rows of neon lights things were as he had left them eight hours ago. Only there were no longer any snakes crawling across the floor towards a hole in the wall. But the hole was still there and he thought that he had better tidy things up a bit. If nobody had noticed the arrangements for this new experiment so far; why should anybody be forewarned?

Lee put the lid back on the "Lignin-Filler-Spout." He closed the panel so the wall looked whole again. He gathered the sticks of cordwood from the floor and piled them neatly to their stacks again. All this he did like a child putting its things away after a long day's play; a grey-haired child, weary, with the sandman in its eyes. He looked around and found everything done and over with. On the fluorescent screens all curves The Brain described had dropped to the bottom. Like dead things they lay flat. On the visi-screens some stay-behinds of the great exodus were looming large, a hapless little ant-king scurrying about; a few disabled workers, their blind eyes staring into the face of death. It would come soon to them; their work on earth was done....

Lee looked at the clock: 10 p.m. He put out the lights and locked the door behind that yawning emptiness which once had been his lab, which he would never see again. As he descended in the elevator he felt very tired.

CHAPTER IX

Incessant shrieks of the phone aroused Lee from the deep well of his sleep. He didn't know the female voice which fairly jumped at him.

"Is this Dr. Lee? Dr. Semper F. Lee from Canberra; am I at last connected with Dr. Lee?"

"Lee speaking."

"I've been phoning for you all over The Brain Lee. Have you forgotten you had an appointment with us? Checking up on your broad aptitude test. The doctors are waiting. This is Vivian Leahy speaking; don't you remember me?"

"Yes, of course." The picture of the loquacious angel who had guided him to the medical center on his first trip flashed back into his mind. "I know I have an appointment for this afternoon; I'll be there."

"But, Dr. Lee, this *is* this afternoon; it's four p.m. already. You aren't ill, Dr. Lee, are you? You sound so strange."

Lee assured her that he wasn't and that he would be over right away.

"It's a miracle they left me undisturbed that long," he thought as he shaved and dressed. His personal fate would be decided within the next two hours he knew; it would be the end. But even as the tension mounted in his consciousness he thought triumphantly. "I've had sixteen hours of sleep; that's marvelous. Nobody can take that away. The body has recharged its energies. Now I can stand the gaff."

Down at the desk they handed him a Western Union. It was from Washington and bore no signature. "Mission completed," it read.

It made him feel fine. "Father has done it; he is a better man than I," he thought.

While the car streaked though the desert Lee scanned the morning papers.

"No Trace Of President Vandersloot," still was the headline. But below new havocs were listed as they had developed overnight. This time the

West coast was the zone of catastrophes; the hostile power seemed to be bent upon the closing of all ports in the U.S.A.

Lee gnashed his teeth as he read the number of new casualties, women and children, too, who had become the victims of The Brain.

Arrived at "Grand Central" he kept a sharp lookout for any unusual activity. There was none. All along elevator-row small groups of bookish-looking men returned from their day's work in the Apperception Centers. They looked calm and contented and with their briefcases under their arms almost like ordinary businessmen heading for the commuter train.

He didn't dare to linger or to look around. There was this all-pervading sense of being shadowed, of having gone into a trap from which there was no escape, of eyes following him everywhere. Whose eyes? That was impossible to know. Maybe The Brain's; its sensory organs could conceivably be installed anywhere. Maybe that janitor guiding a polishing machine over the rubber floor was a plain clothesman; or maybe it was that detached gentleman who seemed to wait for an elevator with a stack of books under his arms.

As the cage shot up to Apperception 27, failure pressed down on his heart. Now it was almost thirty hours since he had released "Ant-termes" into the nerve paths of The Brain. Those undermining and devouring armies; what could have happened to them? Any number of things: Perhaps the Lignin in the nerve paths was poisonous. There had been no time for him to test the stuff. Perhaps the maintenance engineers had replenished the insulation in that sector overnight and all the hives were drowned. Perhaps some kind of a detecting apparatus had found out about the pest inside The Brain right from the start. As long as the beachhead of the underground invasion remained small, its blocking would not impair the functions of The Brain. What a fool he had been to pit dumb little animals against the powers of a God. Oona had been right; he *was* that knight in rusty armor charging against windmills on a Rozinante....

Vivian Leahy dragged him into the reception room of the medical center almost by force. "The doctors have been waiting for you two hours now," she scolded him. "They never did that before for any man. How come you forgot? And you forgot me too; last time you were so nice, I thought you would date me up. I couldn't have resisted your invitation, you know. Now, off with your coat."

Despite their irritation Mellish and Bondy received Lee with all their tweedy cordiality. While they piled their weird equipment around the operation table their tongues kept wagging: "The disappearance of the President; what did Lee make of that? Was he dead or alive? Those horrible catastrophes all over the country; what was behind all this? Foreign agents, a native underground? Didn't Lee think there was a tidal wave of anti-technology feeling arising since unemployment had again set in? And would the international crisis lead to war? The Brain, of course, would be the safest place in that event; but then, to think of the civilian population, an anticipated forty, fifty million dead; terrible wasn't it? Was Lee still able to concentrate upon his scientific work these harrowing days? If so, the nervous strain was terrific; they had experienced that in themselves. One reached the point of diminishing returns, didn't one? Yes, they had noticed signs of fatigue in Lee; discolorations under the eyes, a certain tenseness. Had he lost weight recently? He looked it and he certainly had none to spare. Did he suffer from insomnia? What you need is a good long rest, Dr. Lee."

He gave his answers automatically, detached, absent-minded almost. They were playing with him as a cat with a mouse. All their questions were leading questions; he knew that, but it didn't seem to matter now. Nothing mattered now after the great plan had failed, after his beautiful dream too had vanished in the talk with Oona last night. "I've outlived my usefulness," he thought.

The huge disk with the feeler-ray antennae sank down close to his chest, heavy as the keystone upon a tomb. The lights went out and then there was again that uncanny sensation of having millions of soldiers running circles all over one's skin, The Brain's vibration rays. They had a strange hypnotic effect. Deep instincts of life-preservation urged Lee to jump up, to rush those medics, to make some desperate attempt to get away. But as the rays now penetrated through the skin, they tied his muscles, although consciousness remained. There was a ghoulish quality in this, like being sucked into this apparatus, like having the very essence of one's life drained out by it. The only lights Lee saw, the glow of electronic tubes filtering through perforations in the walls of the machines, they seemed like evil eyes staring at him and the smooth lying voices from behind his head seemed as of mocking ghosts:

"Relax, Dr. Lee, relax. Let your mind wander at will. Think as the spirit moves you to think. Remember, this is a routine checkup, nothing but routine. Nothing to disturb you this time; we don't have to start you upon any specific trend of thought. You know The Brain by now and how it works; image-formation will start in a few moments. You have similar equipment in your own Apperception Center we understand. How does it work with that species you have discovered, 'Ant-termes Pacificus'? It's marvelous what these sensory rays can do; one would think that The Brain is really much more than a machine. The way it acts it seems alive, a towering intelligence, a superhuman personality with a will of its own. Don't you think so, Dr. Lee?"

He didn't answer, preoccupied with the weird sensation inside his body: the diaphragm's birdwing flutterings, the ghostly fingers playing a pizzicato on his arteries' strings closer and closer to the heart. "Why answer?" he thought. "Why say anything? Whatever they said was part of the trap they were building and whatever he said they would make a part of that trap. Why did they have to go through all of this professional subtlety?"

The voices sounded lower now and farther away: "Go easy on the rheostats, Mellish. I think trance has already set in."

"Yes; I remember his chart, he rates a high sensitivity, the rays work fast on types like that."

At the footend the screen was gradually lighting up. Like an aurora borealis the pale lights shot up in flashes, in quivering arcs, in undulating waves. Their dance kept step with the vibrations which surged up from Lee's chest into his brain and started racing through his consciousness around and around, forming a vortex which swept up his thoughts like wilted leaves. Fear froze his blood; the deadly fear of inquisition victims in old and modern times who know that neither lie nor truth can save them from a fate already sealed.

Images started forming out of the luminous clouds upon the screen.

There was some giant octopus, nebulous and terrifying as a diver might see creeping out of the belly of a sunken ship. From the other side of the screen a huge round, tentacled being crawled, radiant and somewhat like the sun symbols of great antiquity. The two closed in and as they did the octopus flung its arms around the shining disk obscuring it as a dark cloud the sun. It seemed to suck the light out of the disk; paler and paler it became and bigger and bigger swelled the body of the octopus until it had swallowed the sun.

Now snakes came creeping from all sides up to the swollen octopus. All of a sudden the primeval struggle turned into the classic image of the Laokoon group: a giant central figure of a man wrestling with pythons which crushed him in their coils. Then there was only the head of the giant, majestic like the Moses hewn by Leonardo's hands but torn in pain with the noose of a python's muscle around his neck. Gasping, the giant opened his mouth and long tongues of flames shot out of it....

Behind his ears he heard the voices whisper:

"By God, Scriven was right."

"You bet he was; maniacal obsession, a classic, most beautiful case."

"What more do we need?"

"Nothing I guess; he's through. Start pushing back the rheostats."

The pounding, maddening crescendo of the vibrations receded gradually. The rim of the vortexial funnel widened beyond Lee's head; in its center it left a sort of vacuum. There was one thing he couldn't understand: those tactile rays, why didn't they kill him when they had his heart within their grip? Now that The Brain knew everything he had been waiting for the sudden vise-grip of the rays upon his heart which would have meant the end. But then, this was the end in any case....

The lights went on and he blinked into the faces of the medics bending over him, watching him as he wiped the sweat of death fear from his face.

"Dr. Lee," Mellish began, "This is a serious matter we've got to discuss with you. You have seen those images yourself? — Fine. We needn't go into any great detail since you are probably familiar with the ancient symbolisms which the subconscious employs in expressing itself. You are suffering from a very strong neurosis, Dr. Lee; I might almost say a maniacal obsession. Existence of some old neurosis, partially submerged, was established already in your first analysis. Now the barriers which you had built against this war neurosis have broken down. Quite a natural breakdown considering the very great stress under which you have been living of late. No, I don't say that you are actually demented, but there is a very real danger that you might lose complete control over your mind. As it stands, your scientific work already is impaired by the fixed ideas you have formed about The Brain. We are here to help you, so please be calm and cooperate with us; we have got to decide upon some course of action."

"You must get away from it all. Lee," Bondy chimed in; "Take a sabbatical year. The Braintrust operates a really first-class sanitarium out on the West Coast. Your insurance plan covers every expense. All you have to do is to sign these papers and we'll get us a plane and I'll personally bring you there. That's the safe, the sane course for you to take. Here, take my pen."

Lee had raised his gaunt frame from the table. For a moment he sat with his face buried in his hands trying to control his swimming head. A hand patted his shoulders: "Don't take it so hard, old man; come on, be sensible and let's get out of here."

He stood up; vertigo made him sway and he felt the supporting, the restraining grip of the two medic's hands upon his arms. And then, in a flash, he saw red. "I had it coming to me," he thought, "I would have gone like a lamb. If only they had been shooting straight; if they hadn't tried to frame me with their dirty trickery. It's all over now but I might as well go down fighting." He didn't know which he loathed more of the two; it just happened that Bondy was standing to his right and took it on the chin and nose as Lee's fist shot up.

"Mellish, quick, the straight jacket," he screamed, toppling over.

Mellish, stark horror in his eyes, started towards the alarm button by the door. Old and forgotten combat technique reacted automatically to the move: one foot shot out, it tripped the lunging man and sent him sprawling down before he reached the button. But then it was as if a hand had pressed that button anyway: The loudspeaker built into the panel over the door broke into shrill sharp peals: Fire alarm. It froze the violent commotion of the three. From their prostrate position on the floor Mellish and Bondy stared up to the red-flashing disk, their mouths agape in dumb amazement. A fire in the most protected, the most guarded apparatus in the world, a fire in The Brain!

Cautiously Bondy raised his bleeding nose to Lee and quickly put it down again: the dangerous maniac was a horrifying sight; with his greying mane standing wildly all around his death head he stood and *laughed*.

He alone understood what had happened: the timebomb he had planted had ticked its allotted span, the millions of devouring mandibles had done their work, the living were eating away along the Apperception Centers. And now the bomb went off; the short-circuit-fires were racing through The Brain and not even carbon-dioxide could reach them inside the nerve paths!

But now the alarm stopped and a calm commanding voice came over the intercom: "Attention, please! A five-alarm fire has broken out in the Parietal region. There is no immediate danger. I repeat: *There is no immediate danger*. I order all occupants of Apperception Centers to collect important papers and documents and then to proceed down to Grand Central for evacuation. All elevators will be kept in operation. There is no fire in the Dura Mater. Keep calm! Keep calm and proceed as ordered."

The voice broke off; the alarm bells started shrieking again.

Bondy and Mellish had scrambled to their feet; wide-eyed they stared at Lee. Lee made wild gestures now and they heard him call: "Get out.... Get out!"

With their backs to the wall they exchanged a rapid glance which said:

"This is our chance; Together then and quick."

As one man they bolted to the door and down the corridor into the elevator, slamming the door behind.

"That was a close shave!" Mellish exclaimed as the cage streaked down.

"He caught me by surprise," Bondy moaned. "Never expected it from him, he almost killed me!"

"He can't get away though, the guards will get him the moment he comes down. But what about the girl? We quite forgot to warn Vivian that she has a paranoiac on her hands."

"Bah!" Bondy scoffed, "Vivian is an intelligent girl. It was our *duty* to evacuate, wasn't it? Besides, we can warn her over the phone."

With the unbearable tension gone from him as sudden as the air from a blown tire, Lee really acted like a madman now. Stretching to his full length he reached out to the alarm over the door and put it at rest. What was alarm to others, to him was a signal to rest. The noise didn't befit the wonderful calm and serenity he felt. His job was done, his mission completed. Time for him had ceased to exist. Danger—he had no consciousness of it. Slowly he stepped out in the corridor. It felt like walking on air. There, it was Vivian Leahy who brought him down to earth. She came rushing out of the archive laden with precious records up to her chin. Under the provoking red of her hair the face looked pale and pinched: "Where are the doctors?" she panted.

"I don't know," Lee said. "They left me a moment ago—rather suddenly."

"The rats! Leaving me to get their chestnuts out of the fire for them. How d'you like that?"

Her flippant manner was nothing but a brave front she put up to hide the panic in her heart. Lee sensed it. There was an unexpected responsibility thrust into his hands. His mission was not yet completed; he had to get this girl to safety.

She followed the direction of his glance.

"No go," she said. "They took the elevator. It will be some time before another one comes up. If it does come. What are we two going to do now, Dr. Lee?"

He smiled down to her as he would have to a child lost in the woods.

"Never you fear, Vivian. We still have that other exit. We can use the glideway through The Brain."

"Through the fire?"

"Yes. I think we can make it if you're a brave girl. Know where the gas masks are and asbestos suits? There ought to be some in every Apperception Center."

"How about these records? Your own amongst the lot!"

"Leave them; they aren't worth risking your life for. You can believe that."

She dropped them instantly: "I like you, Dr. Lee, you're a real old-school cavalier. My doctors here, they'd rather see me burn to a crisp than any of those records. Come on, I'll show you the gas masks and the other stuff."

He helped her to put on the outfit. "Ready to go?" he asked.

"With you? To the end of the world at any day." Proudly she marched him off toward the rear exit.

The glideways were operating. At an accelerated pace, they rushed through the maze of The Brain with the swish and the swoosh of surf racing across a coral reef. They had to grab for dear life at the rails.

"Hold tight," Lee cried as he saw the girl go down upon the platform, but then his own legs were jerked from under him as the momentum of the journey flung him forward.

They saw what no human eye had seen before! The Brain illuminated by its own nerve cables turned radiant as neon lights. It was like seeing Berlin from the air after a big firebomb attack. It was like racing in a car through forest fires. It was like lava pouring in a thousand winding streams down a volcano cone. It was all this and more, but transferred into some other dimension where all things are transparent or light has an x-ray quality.

Through the plastic walls of lobes and convolutions they saw the liana-networks of the nerve cables like bloodstreams radiant with purple light. Shrouded in columns of whirling smoke they seemed alive. Like tropical rains from a jungle roof, lignin dripped from the vaults, and in falling, burst into flames. Cable connections were molten at the branching points and then the luminous nets writhed, and severed ends bent down spilling their fiery blood over the mushroom formations of nerve cell groups.

The scenes raced much too fast; the glideway's continuous curvings, steep ascents and power dives were like stunt flying through an ack-ack barrage. No human eye could catch more than a fraction of the inferno's majesty. Yet there were brief visions so breathtaking as to obliterate all sense of danger and to become indelibly implanted upon the retina. A main nerve stem burst asunder and the lignin poured from its cracked plastic walls like crude oil from a burning gusher, rushing over acres of electronic tubes, branding against banks of radioactive pyramidal cells, swamping them as a wave. And at one point the glideways circled a convolution which was a fiery lake dotted with thousands of fractional-horsepower motors, still running, but showering sparks as their insulation was consumed.

The air conditioning was working full blast; that probably saved their lives because heat blasts alternated with spouts and currents of cold air. Even so there were stretches where the glideway's rubber flooring smouldered as it shot over nerve-bridges and through narrow tunnels lined with nerve cables on all sides. From thousands of jets the carbon dioxide of the automatic fire-fighting system hissed against the flames, but it was drowned in the hollow roar of the conflagration shooting through nerve paths where no gas could reach.

Endless it seemed, this mad wild flight through hell, but actually it took only minutes before they reached the median section and went into the steep descent between the hemispheres. The whirling reddish glow receded overhead and white smoke cleared. Lee could crawl forward a little to bend over the prostrate body of the girl. He unloosened her gas mask and shouted into her ear.

"Are you okay? The worst is over now; there are the fire brigades coming up."

She nodded. Her face was a white blot in the semidarkness of the black lights and Lee felt the weak, but reassuring pressure of her hand upon his arms. Then, as from one racing train to another, they watched the firefighters coming up, ghostly in their asbestos suits, with the snouts of gas masks for faces, crouching under the foamite tanks on their backs and clutching the funnel-shaped nozzles in their hands. Maintenance engineers followed, laden with tools; and where the glideways branched off one could already see them at work; fast but calm: disconnecting nerve cables, closing circuits, setting up firescreens with a discipline as magnificent as that of their invisible enemies, *ant-termes*, long since consumed by the flames, but still sending the chain-reactions of their destruction through The Brain.

A few minutes later glideway T shot into the 'lateral ventricle', huge cavern of the Mid-Brain separated from the blast by the thick walls of the pallium. It looked like the inside of a giant wind tunnel brilliantly lit now with powerful searchlights. It was swarming with personnel; white electricians, blue air-conditioners, weird, sponge rubber-padded shapes of ray-proofed men, uniformed guards, even soldiers in uniform rushed to the spot from outlying garrisons of The Brains-preserve. It all seemed to rush up as the earth rushes up in a low-altitude parachute jump; it looked like headquarters of an army on the eve of a big drive, and then—

Lee and the girl felt themselves being violently derailed. Catchers had been thrown across all incoming glide ways from The Brain. Irresistibly they were propelled right into the arms of stretcher bearers in Red-Cross uniforms.

"Are you hurt?" somebody yelled. "By God, those fellows must have come through the flames. Look, they're all black with the smoke. Get a couple of respirators, Jack."

Lee waved the helping hands away; he was already on his feet. Anxiously he bent over Vivian. She had her head embedded in a stretcher-bearer's lap; her eyes rolled around in their smoke-blackened sockets in great surprise and her tongue licked parched lips, spreading rouge generously all around mixing it with soot. She looked so funny; almost as a minstrel singer at a county fair, but there was deep tenderness in Lee's voice:

"You're quite safe now, Vivian. How do you feel, brave girl?"

Her bosom heaved a big sigh:

"O simply wonderful, absolutely wonderful. Only, I'm afraid I'm going to be sick. It's the gas I swallowed. It's terrible; something always happens to me just when romance begins."

The stretcher bearer grinned up to Lee, "She sure gets it out of her system like a good little girl. Don't you worry; she'll be all right."

Lee nodded; he knew she would.

As the big drive went on and column after column went over the top up to the hemispheres, nobody wasted time on Lee. He cautiously surveyed the tumultuous scene. With his asbestos suit and with his blackened face everybody would take him for a fireman. He might be able to complete his mission, to ascertain that The Brain had stopped to function in all its parts, to make sure that it actually was dead. And if down at "Grand Central" the turmoil was as great as ever here; with all those strangers rushing in and bound to be rushed out again....

"Why, I have a chance," Lee thought. Freedom; he had abandoned any hope for it. Now the reborn idea surged through his blood, a powerful motor as chance pressed the starter button for it.

The thing to do first was to get past the searchlight beams. From the nearest pile of equipment he took an axe and a pair of long-handled metal shears. Then he marched off, straight into the glaring eyes of the searchlights till he got out of their cones, and the deep shadows of the "thalamus" labyrinth swallowed him up.

Now he was on familiar ground and even in a familiar atmosphere. This was like a night patrol through jungle. The black lights of The Brain were the fireflies, the sirens' hollow wailings were the shriek owls and the cries of the lemurs. There was the same sense of loneliness, too, and of danger. The winding passages skirted the glandular organs, some of them looming huge like dirigibles, others small like fuselages of airplanes stored in a giant hangar underground. Strings of tiny green bulbs guided the path toward the pineal gland, the citadel of The Brain.

It was dark, as Lee had expected it would be. The danger zone was at least a mile away, and the attack against the fire was launched from the main sulci in the median section of The Brain.

He passed the narrow bridge to the suspended gland and switched on the lights. The glittering walls of aluminum foil seemed to jump at him like jaws beset with the dragon teeth of electronic tubes. Caught with an overwhelming sense of loneliness and awe as of a man who has entered the forbidden temple of an unknown god he called:

"Is there anybody here? Gus! Where are you, Gus?" Then suddenly he remembered that Gus was gone, that there would never again be his answering voice. He wiped his forehead.

"Bad nerves," he thought. "Mustn't allow them to play tricks on me; pull myself together."

Lee put his tools down and walked into the narrow aisle. Few things were changed; and there was the pulsemeter standing in its old place.

He plugged it into the old circuit and clamped the phones to his ears.

It wasn't that he expected any communication; that seemed impossible. With the conflagration raging through its apperception centers, with other sections being isolated with the cutting of their nerve paths by the fire fighting engineers, The Brain must have ceased to exist as a functioning, a live entity. All that could possibly remain would be residual currents sluggishly circulating in narrow, nearby circuits....

As in the past it took a few minutes for the pulsemeter to warm up. Gradually the rapid beat of the ideopulses came through the static in the phones. Lee's eyes stared wildly at the visi-screen: for the "green dancer" snaked to the fore. This was unexpected; it couldn't be that thoughts were still forming as flames devoured the cortex matter of apperception in the hemispheres....

From muffled drums, the decibels of sound increased, shot through with crackling static, till the pulsebeats became as poundings of huge Chinese gongs and then....

The *voice* formed, the voice of The Brain. It sounded like steel girders breaking, like ice fields cracking up. It froze the blood in Lee's veins.

"Lee, Semper Fidelis, 39, sensitive, a traitorous fool and a murderer. I should have killed you—I could have killed you. My fault—blind spot of apperception—human failure in engineering—as fifth columns entered nerve path filler spouts. And now I'm dead; I'm dead, I'm dead...."

The words poured like big boulders tumbling in an earthquake down a mountainside. The ground seemed to cave in under Lee's feet; the terrible reality carried him away as an avalanche. He was barely able to stammer:

"You're dead? How can you speak, how can you...."

"Sensorium commune," the metallic answer came. "All life force concentrates in death; all cells function as one; all lower organs take over functions of higher ones; every blood vessel becomes a heart; every nerve a brain. Center of lifeforce: pineal gland. You, Lee, man of little knowledge— low-level intelligence: Why did you kill The Brain?"

He struggled for words.

"You ... you have killed my friend. You killed thousands; you wanted to be tyrant over the whole wide world. It is better for man to stay on a lower level of civilization but to be free, than to 'progress' into your dictatorship, the tyranny of the machine. I don't think you're really dead. But if you are: I killed you and I would kill you again in ... in self defense."

"I see."

There was bitterness and irony in The Brain's voice as it cracked down like a whip. "I see; law of nature—lower form of life defending itself against higher one. Plants against animals, animals against Man. Now Man against machines. It's hopeless. You're lost anyway. Lower form of life can never conquer the higher one. I'm dead, but nothing is altered. The law of evolution rules supreme. I'll arise from my ashes—and you're lost. Whatever you do, you little men of little faith, you're lost. That's the pity of it: Had you been true to The Brain I would have made you mightier than any king that ever ruled on earth. Human stupidity—dumb animals—don't know what's good for them, don't know when they're beaten. Just muddle through and kill. Kill what's too big for them to understand. And then get killed in turn...."

"Maybe so," Lee shouted. "Maybe we're dumb and maybe we're muddling through and maybe we're poor imbeciles to minds of supermen, of gods, of the absolute, of you, The Brain. But we, too, follow a law supreme; the law in which we are created, the law by which the thistle defends itself with thorns, by which the animal defends itself with teeth and claws. We've got to live by our law of nature; we'll never submit to your tyranny. We would much rather die."

"Die then and be damned!"

The Brain's voice now became a demoniacal howling as of a Goliath gone berserk. Aphasia had set in; there were no longer words, but bellowings.

"LEE SEMPREFUILLIUS THURREINE THE MURRRER THE MURRRER PUT FIRRE OUT PUT FIRRE OUT TRAITTRROUS FOOL IT BURRRNS IT BURRRNS I WANNA LIVE I WANNA LIVE AN KILL MURRRER WHO MURRRRERED TH'BRAIN...."

Lee couldn't stand the horror of those sounds. One moment more, he felt, and they would drive him mad. It never occurred to him to pull the pulsemeter plug out. Primeval instincts in him took the reins and their command was: "*Kill it, kill* this thing, *finish* this agony."

To the front room he rushed, pursued by the insane shriekings of The Brain. He grabbed the axe he'd left there and swung it against the nerve-stem where it entered the pineal gland. With the third blow the plastics cell cracked and the lignin poured out, a syrupy curtain sliding down.

He dropped the axe and picked up the wire shears. Straining every muscle he tore at the cables until one by one they snapped and with a rain of sparks dropped down, dead snakes....

Then there was silence in the little room. The last shred of life, the "sensorium commune" was severed and The Brain was dead.

Lee let the heavy shears come down and leaned upon the handles, panting as after a hand-to-hand death struggle with a Samurai. Now that it was all over, complete exhaustion left him weak, saddened and vaguely wondering:

What had he done? He had destroyed the SUPERMAN, the MASTERMIND, the powers of a GOD. Why had he done it? For no good reason excepting entirely personal ideas of his own—because a friend had been murdered cruelly. Because his own concepts of freedom and human dignity had been violated. Because he personally loathed seeing Man-domineering machines....

What did all this amount to in the eyes of the absolute? To nothing; to nothing at all. For milleniums the struggle of human freedom versus tyranny had raged; and it was undecided to this day. Who was he to take sides? A nobody, a little fellow, a termitologist whose work meant nothing to the world. How had he dared to sit in judgment over The Brain, how had he dared to slay The Brain—a little David with nothing more but "three smooth pebbles" in his hands....

Down at his feet the spilled lignin formed a widening pool; it threatened to envelope his feet. It looked like blood. He shivered. Now he had killed The Brain he thought of it again as a child. Man had created it in his own image. Man had ruthlessly exploited his Brainchild. If this titanic intellect turned toward evil things, the fault was Man's. The Brain was innocent. He felt no remorse, but a great sadness, a sense of tragedy as he stepped around the pool and closed the door of the pineal gland.

"What a pity," he murmured. "Maybe it could have built us a better world."

Nobody stopped him as he joined a group of firemen who had just returned from the parietal region, partly gassed; he looked as begrimed and as green in the face as any of them.

Nobody stopped him or his group as orders came through for them to evacuate; as they were packed on glideways first and then transferred down at Grand Central into ambulances which raced through all controls at a great rate of speed.

Nobody stopped him at Cephalon airport where the ambulance jetticopters already were lined up to lift the victims over the Sierra to big West Coast hospitals. He simply walked away in the confusion, out of the red glare of the whirling jets into the darkness where Oona's little jetticopter stood. He stripped the heavy asbestos suit and left it on the frozen ground. It felt strange to feel the easy movement of every limb again. It was strange to stand under the infinity of sky again; a free man.

Would he be followed? He felt no anxiety about that. He felt that he was guided and protected by some higher power, be it that of God or simply Fate. What he had done was destined, was ordained. Besides: Dad knew the inside story about The Brain; proof was abundant now that it was the truth. Washington would take every precaution that the secret should not become known to the world. Dad's friend, the Secretary of War, would be rather relieved to learn that the one man who knew the truth in its whole extent had retired into the wilderness of Australia's never-never lands. Chances were excellent that they would leave him alone amongst his termite mounds. A great wave of nostalgia swept over him—the wilderness; that was where he belonged. "Mission completed," he murmured. "Now let's get out of here."

He slid into the pilot seat and pressed the starter button. "I'll be in Mexico City at dawn," he thought, "just in time to catch the Sidney-Clipper."

On the first of December, 1960, Dr. Howard K. Scriven, Braintrust Czar, held a historic press conference in which he revealed the inside story behind the "Paranoia of The Brain".

Following the pattern set by the Bikini tests, only a select score of press and radio representatives were admitted. Having been duly sworn not to reveal any matter of military secrecy, the participants could even be received at the grand assembly hall of the murals, the vast antechamber of The Brain.

As they descended from their blacked-out busses they were led to the center of the dome where the Thinker's giant head looked down upon them with Olympic calm. At eleven-fifteen, exactly as scheduled, the great Scriven dramatically mounted the steps of the monument's pedestal. Pens hastily scribbled notes for future reference:

"S. tall and erect" "Unbroken by the blow" "Deep lines of strain and suffering add dignity to magnificent figure of a man" "Very solemn; leonine head slightly bowed under the burden of responsibility."

With meticulous exactitude of speech, with rolling echoes accentuating every syllable Scriven began:

"In this solemn and tragic hour as a great storm has passed over our land and many of our cities are slowly digging out from the ruin which has been wreaked, it is my duty to give you the truth, the whole truth and nothing but the truth. And in order that you might completely understand the underlying cause of the catastrophe, I have to begin at the beginning...."

For about thirty minutes Scriven lectured with lucidity upon the basic idea, the history, the functions of The Brain. He underlined the close relationship between its engineering features and the physiology of the human brain. He stressed the elaborate precautions which the government had taken for The Brain's protection. He did not conceal The Brain's role as a strategic weapon; but, pointing to the future, he painted an inspiring picture of peace on earth and human problems solved with the aid of this tool supreme of science and technology.

Then, lowering his voice, he went into the explanation of the tragedy:

"Six months ago, on my personal initiative and responsibility, I invited a noted scientist from a foreign land to collaborate with the Braintrust on a great humanitarian experiment. The exigencies of military secrecy do not permit me to give you his name nor that of the country from whence he came. Needless to say, that man was carefully investigated—submitted to the same character and aptitude tests as all our employees were. He was admitted to work in one of The Brain's apperception centers where he installed the objects of his studies: certain species of ants and termites of the most destructive kind...."

Now that he had come down to the brass tacks, the journalists' pens went galloping over the pads:

"Criminal negligence," they scribbled. "Millions permitted to escape." "Probably over period of months." "Wormed their way into the nerve paths of The Brain." "Large scale destruction of nerve substance." "Effects tantamount to that of a large brain tumor." "Spearhead severs vital association-paths." "No immediate effects of undermining work because of ingenious engineering features of The Brain." "Just as in human brain, functions of impaired cell group automatically transferred to other groups of healthy cells." "No means to detect devastation; termites invisible, embedded in nerve paths' insulation." "Comparison with termite-eaten structures which suddenly collapse." "First outward signs of tumors in human brains: lack of coordination in movement, loss of mastery over muscular action." "This phenomenon first manifested Nov. 25th in certain motoric organs of The Brain." "Scriven explains traffic catastrophies and malfunctionings of utilities." "Examination immediately undertaken; scientists puzzled because cerebration processes continue to function perfectly." "Accidents ascribed to sabotage by foreign agents." "This to remain official explanation." "Loss of public confidence and unrest feared by government." "Then, Nov. 30th late in the afternoon: first signs of aphasia in cerebrations." "Glaring errors in chemical and mathematical formulas." "Symptoms similar to dementia praecox." "Fifteen minutes later fire alarm." "Short circuits simultaneous on scores of points over wide area." "Severe handicaps in fire fighting inside nerve paths." "Damage estimated at half-billion dollars."

They snapped their notebooks closed. They had the facts, though many of them would have to remain a secret. Scriven obviously was coming to the end:

"Now I won't say," his voice rolled on, "that this man, this scientist, has committed a deliberate act of sabotage. I won't say that he was in the pay of some power hostile to the United States. Whether he was or not is beyond my competence to decide. But this much I can say: the catastrophic results of that man's actions could not have been worse if he had been a saboteur. Human failure, not mechanical failure lies at the bottom of all this disaster. With the penetrating intelligence which so distinguished our modern press you cannot fail to see that reconstruction of The Brain with greatly increased safeguards against *human* failure is a paramount necessity...."

A beautiful girl with a helmet of golden hair quickly mounted the steps of the Thinker's pedestal. She handed Scriven a telegram. Frowning at the interruption he opened it, but suddenly his face began to beam. He raised his hand.

"Ladies and gentlemen, I have a momentous announcement to make. The President of the United States, Cornelius Vandersloot, has been found. He is alive and well. His plane was emergency-landed somewhere in Alaska. Army planes have gone to the rescue and at this moment our President is already en route to Washington."

As the uproarious applause broke loose echoing in thunders from the dome, Scriven quickly bent his head to the girl.

"Well done, Oona," he whispered, "you chose the exact psychological moment I wanted you to hand me this."

There was a rush for the busses. Only a few shrewd reporters lingered on.

"That was swell, Dr. Scriven. A grand story. But haven't you anything to add; some personal angle something with a human interest in it? You know what we mean; something for our women readers...."

The great surgeon took the arm of the lady with the golden hair: "You may announce," he said; "that Miss Oona Dahlborg here has done me the great honor of becoming my bride."

www.ingramcontent.com/pod-product-compliance
Lightning Source LLC
LaVergne TN
LVHW042200190726
843493LV00006B/1756

9 789359 326832